Suffer the Children

Suffer the Children

Dispatches to and from
the Front Line

ANDREW WHITE

continuum

Published by the Continuum International Publishing Group
The Tower Building, 11 York Road, London SE1 7NX
80 Maiden Lane, Suite 704, New York NY 10038

www.continuumbooks.com

Copyright © Andrew White, 2010

Drawings in the second plate section are by Havan Hamid Majid, aged 15,
a Mandean member of the congregation of St George's, Baghdad:

1. The Virgin of Iraq
2. Jesus sweating blood in Gethsemane
3. Suffering the little children . . .
4. Terrorists attacking a school
5. Bomb damage, with St George's in the background
6. The Crucifixion
7. Fetching water from a standpipe
8. American soldiers on patrol
9. Planting a flower of peace
10. The Ascension

First published 2010

British Library Cataloguing-in-Publication Data
A catalogue record for this book is available from the British Library.

ISBN 978-1-8470-6374-8

Designed and typeset by Kenneth Burnley, Wirral, Cheshire
Printed and bound by the MPG Books Group

Contents

List of Illustrations

Section 2 (between pages 80 & 81)

Foreword

Yet again my dear friend Andrew White has touched my heart with his unique perspective on children. I was reminded of Charles Dickens' book *A Tale of Two Cities*, a story of the French Revolution:

> Each day, a grim procession of prisoners made its way on the streets of Paris to the guillotine. One prisoner, Sidney Carton, a brave man who had once lost his soul but had now found it again, was now giving his life for his friend. Beside him there was a young girl. They had met before in the prison, and the girl had noticed the man's gentleness and courage. She said to him, 'If I may ride with you, will you let me hold your hand? I am not afraid, but I am little and weak, and it will give me more courage.'
>
> So they rode together, her hand in his; and when they reached the place of execution, there was no fear in her eyes. She looked up into the quiet, composed face of her companion, and said, 'I think you were sent to me by heaven.'

I believe this can be said of Canon Andrew White. He is a big man; he is astute, alert, passionate and compassionate – and, deep down, a little child! As Dickens also said:

> It is good to be children sometimes, and never better than at Christmas, when its mighty founder was a child Himself.

J. John (Canon)
March 2010

*To all my children in England and Iraq
and the many young friends who keep me going:*

*Josiah and Jacob, David, Lena, Alan, Angelina, Bashir,
Fulla, Kristin, Lina, Mabel, Maher, Mardina, Mariam,
Mariam, Martin, Mona, Nahrain, Sally, Sandra, Sandy,
Sandy, Stephani and Yusif, Havan, Johnson, Despina,
Roni, Josiah, Emily and Nathanael, Micaiah, Anna,
Jacob and Samuel, Destiny, Sophia and Judah,
Rebecca and Nicholas, Gloria, Willie and David,
Breanna and all the children at St George's, Baghdad*

Acknowledgements

This is a book about the little people who inspire me. There is nothing complicated about it, and yet for some reason it has been one of the hardest things I have written.

I want to thank my editor, Huw Spanner, who has done wonders in pulling it all together. I must also thank Caroline Chartres, my commissioning editor, for her immense patience and endless encouragement. If it had not been for her, I would have given up the task. I am also indebted to my young assistant Micaiah Norby. Without her, this book would never have been finished.

I want to thank all those who have contributed to this book in their own words, from Baghdad, Bethlehem, Charlotte and Jerusalem, and not least my own sons, Josiah and Jacob. Finally, I am especially grateful to Havan for her pictures, which always inspire me.

Canon Andrew White
Baghdad, February 2010

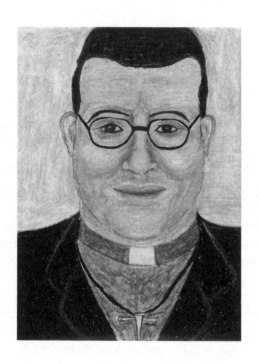

Introduction

People often ask me how I manage to keep going, working amidst the violence and fear of Iraq and even winning prizes and awards for what I accomplish there. They know I suffer from multiple sclerosis and am not in the best of health. A lot of people are puzzled by this question, and I don't think that anyone ever guesses the answer. It is the children who sustain me, children who love me and children I love. Whether they are with me in person or they just communicate with me by e-mail, phone or text, often they are the source of whatever wisdom, whatever spiritual insight I may have.

Many of them have suffered a great deal, but that does not prevent them from being channels for the love of the Almighty. Most of them are in Baghdad, but there are some in Bethlehem, too, and one in Jerusalem, and then a whole crowd of young people in Charlotte, in North Carolina. In this book I want to look at these three groups of children, in Iraq, Israel/Palestine and America, and how they help me and support me. There is a hidden power in these young people that is the power of God, and it is a power we all need to explore.

As I write this, I am on the plane to Baghdad. This city is the place I love most in the world, though it is one of the world's most troubled and troublesome places. Here I will be working with some extremely difficult and even dangerous people, as I try to secure the release of hostages and continue the search for peace with people who sometimes seem to want only war. However, soon will come the highlight of my week when, surrounded by heavily armed soldiers, I go to church. As we arrive at St George's, I will be met by scores of children shouting '*Abuna, Abuna*!' ('Father, Father!'). I will hug each one of them and kiss them each three times, and then as I enter God's house I will take off my body armour and hand it to the children and they in turn will hand me my robes. They will kiss my stole – my ecclesiastical scarf – in just the place that I do, and put it round my neck, and then they will walk with me singing up the aisle.

At times like this, I forget the pain outside. The sound of the gunfire no longer disturbs me. All I am conscious of is that I am with my people. I am surrounded by the ones who enable me to keep going, the ones who give me strength. I look at them all in wonder. There is David, of course, and Fulla standing next to me, Yusif in his wheelchair and Lina singing in the choir. These young people have all been through so much. I give them all I have to give, but it doesn't compare with what they give me. Like most children who have grown up in a war zone, they have a special faith and insight. Their desires are so different from those of so many in the West. They know that each day they survive is a miracle, a godsend. Some of them have lost parents, some have lost homes; they know what it means to go without, and yet I never hear from them one word of complaint. Often they have almost nothing – and yet they have everything, because they have a child's faith in a wonderful God.

Next week, my church leaders will come to meet with me at a hotel in the international Green Zone. Walking all the way, and passing through several security checks, they will be accompanied as always by children, who know that their elders are coming to see me and want to come too. They sit or stand quietly for a couple of hours while the adults discuss business, and then it is time for them to talk with me and tell me more of their stories. These young people have no idea what else I do. The fact that I have just come from seeing the prime minister means nothing to them. To them, I am simply their father, and not just in the ecclesiastical sense. Those who have learned a little English call me 'Daddy'. And as far as they are concerned only two things really matter: that their *abuna* loves them and that they love him.

In my training and my early ministry, I heard a lot about children and the need to respect them, protect them and honour them.[1] What I was never told, however, was that they could be your inspiration, or that they could give you so much insight into the teachings of our Lord. I learned all of this once I got to know children who were suffering, who had lived with violence and turmoil and fear, though it took

---

1   I should say that I am constantly aware of our child-protection laws – laws that I totally respect, though at times they can make life difficult. I never see children on their own, without another adult present, and I always keep the door open, though they keep trying to close it. I explain to them why these things have to be so, and they always understand. However, one rule that I cannot obey in Baghdad, though I do in Britain, is that I must not give a child anything. In Iraq, you often have no choice!

me longer to learn that other children, in more tranquil surroundings, also have much to teach us.

In this book I am going to tell the stories of some of these children – children I love as I love my own sons, children from whom I have learned so much. Most of them live in the places of conflict where I work, but not all: some of them live in a very peaceful part of America, and yet they, too, help me to carry my burdens as they pray for me and encourage me. I am constantly aware that my own sons often suffer so that I can do my work, and they, too, give me hope and courage. They never complain (though my wife is careful not to let them see on the television pictures of Baghdad and the kind of conditions I live in). They see photographs of the others and often ask after them, and all the children send each other drawings and presents. I often long that they could all have lives like my own boys', though that will never be; but we live in hope that one day at least they may all have peace.

So, come with me and meet these wonderful children. Witness their love for the Almighty, and their trust in him. Learn with me what Jesus meant when he said, 'Let the little children come to me,' and reflect on his reasons for saying that 'unless you become like little children, you will never enter the kingdom of heaven'.

CHAPTER 1

A Curious Childhood

Once upon a time, I was a child, too. I remember my childhood well and I have always thought that it was pretty unexceptional, but I suppose that actually it was quite eccentric in many ways.

I lived originally in Wanstead, a middle-class enclave in a working-class area of north-east London. My father was Her Majesty's Inspector of Taxes for Woolwich, Bromley and central London. He was very much a Calvinist, very theologically minded and quite academic. His principal mentor in life was the great evangelical preacher and teacher Dr Martyn Lloyd-Jones. My upbringing was very Calvinistic: everything had been planned by God and you were either one of the Elect or you weren't (and I was told that I was). Actually, my parents were not only Strict Baptists but also Pentecostals, which was a very unusual combination, and a really odd mix. My mother's father had been an assistant to Smith Wigglesworth, one of the great pioneers of the Pentecostal movement in Britain, and I still have in my possession the big, leather-bound Bible that 'the Apostle of Faith' read and annotated every day.

To this day, I still think of my parents as 'Mummy' and 'Daddy'. They showered me and my sister and brother with love and gave us all their attention. They also taught us to love Jesus, and I cannot remember a time when I didn't. In fact, I used to pray every day that I would love Jesus more – as I still do. As a child, I used to worry that I had never had 'a conversion experience', but today I give thanks for that, because it is something I have in common with almost all of my people in Baghdad. I was always devout. I always loved going to church and to Sunday school and was always happy to talk about God. I never once doubted my faith. The people around me may have done so – especially much later, when I was at theological college in Cambridge – but I never did, and to this day never have.

One of my earliest memories is of being read John Bunyan's classics *The Pilgrim's Progress* and *The Holy War* when I was six or seven. When Pilgrim comes to the Palace Beautiful, he is asked by Prudence, 'By what means do you find your annoyances, at times, as if they were vanquished?' and he says: 'When I look upon my broidered coat, that will do it; when I look at the book that I carry in my bosom, that will do it; when I think of what I saw at the cross, that will do it; and when I think whither I am going, that will do it.' Those words are still very important to me. When I think about what God has given me, the Bible and the Cross and the fact that I am going to heaven, those are the things that keep me going, even now in Baghdad.

One thing that did bother me as a child was the fact that my brother and sister didn't look like me. They had straight hair and very pale complexions, whereas my hair was curly and I was dark, like my father. He was a product of the British Raj, born in India of Anglo-Indian stock going back maybe a hundred years. Years later, when I started working in the Middle East, I realized that this, too, was a gift from God, because I look much the same as the people I live with and work with, and for this, too, I give thanks. I don't recall being teased because of my colour when I was a child, but as an adult I was once startled to be asked, by a dentist's receptionist, 'Do they have enough to eat where you come from?' She was being quite serious, though I have no idea what prompted her to ask that.

I was quite a happy boy, with a good sense of humour, but I have very little recollection of ever playing with toys. I do remember a chemistry set and one day, when I was eight, causing an explosion in the greenhouse which set it on fire. I can also recall, at the age of ten, dressing up as a policeman and going to stand guard at the Jewish cemetery at the end of our road for over an hour at a time. My father had always taught me to love the Jews, and had also told me about anti-Semitism. So, while other children were playing together, I was spending time standing guard at a cemetery. I wasn't unsporty, however. I used to do the high jump and I remember that when I was 4 foot 7 I could jump my own height, which is really impressive.

I don't think I would have been regarded as precocious, and I wasn't considered to be clever, unlike my sister (who is two years older than me) and my brother, who was a year younger than me. (My brother especially was really intelligent, and far more serious than I was, though he was also quite athletic and when he was 11 or 12 he got into competitive weightlifting and football.) However, when I was ten I started going with my father to Foyles, the famous bookshop in London's Charing Cross Road, and while he was looking at the theology books I would go down to the basement to browse in the medical section. The thing that really interested me was anaesthetics. Today when I ask my son Josiah whether he thinks this is weird, he says he's been told that if you want to make a lot of money, anaesthetics is a good thing to go into; but that wasn't what appealed to me. Someone had told me that anaesthesia is really the thing that keeps people alive during operations and so it is very important.

I had already read my first book on the subject when I told my teacher in primary school that I wanted to be an anaesthetist when I grew up. (I also said that I wanted to be a priest, and she told me I couldn't be both.) Throughout my childhood I carried on reading about anaesthetics – I used to order books from the local library and they had to send off for them. When eventually I did go and study it at St Thomas' Hospital in London, I found I already knew everything we were supposed to learn in the first year. I also joined the St John Ambulance Brigade when I was ten, and once a week I would go to a nearby school to learn first aid with them. I had copious supplies of ointments and bandages and soon I was the person the other local children would come to whenever they hurt themselves.

It was around the same time that I began to visit a woman called Hilda who lived opposite us. She was in her seventies and was bedridden and really couldn't do much for herself at all, and so I would go over and do things for her. Again, I'm not sure why this so appealed to me. She needed my help and that was part of it, though I don't think my parents would have described me as a particularly helpful child. It got me out of the house. Also, she was a devout High Anglican and I had never really met one of those before and she had a lot to teach me about liturgies and hierarchies, which were all very strange to me.

The local priest used to come and see her each week to give her Holy Communion and I was often there when he came, and it wasn't long before I started going to his church – and not just on Sundays. Every day I would run home from school so that I could hear him say evensong from the Book of Common Prayer. Usually I was the only other person present, and the priest soon became a friend. My time was now divided between school and church and Hilda's bedside.

When I was 12, we moved to Bexley, where outer London borders on Kent. Up until then, I had gone to a local state school but now I went to a grant-aided Huguenot school called Picardy Academy. By now, I was interested largely in old people. I went to the local volunteer bureau and they gave me the address of the pop-in parlour and the names of some people to visit. One of these was the wife of an old retired general who had been in the Indian Army. When he died, I used to visit her constantly. I didn't have any close friends of my own age. The thing was that everything I was doing and thinking, my faith and my inter-est in medicine, was so *alien* to most other children. I did none of the things that were expected of the young. All I wanted to do, apart from going to church, doing first aid and reading yet more books on anaesthetics, was to be with my elderly friends. The amount that I did for them – tidying up, making them refreshments, even doing the cleaning – was phenomenal.

I was now going to three different churches on Sundays: the United Reformed church in the morning, the Baptist church in the afternoon and, in the evening, the Pentecostal Assemblies of God church where my parents worshipped. I also went to the URC youth group on Monday evenings, though it was never really my cup of tea. I also found another Anglican church to go to from time to time. It wasn't nearly as high as Hilda's had been, but it seemed to hold together all the elements that the other three church traditions offered.

At school I was bullied a little, though not on account of my colour. I must have seemed very strange to my peers. I was never prepared to do anything naughty and was always quick to tell other children off when they did. I was very attached to my briefcase and I was always very smart – I was known for wearing a three-piece suit at the weekend. One of the elders at the Baptist church had a tailor's shop and I used to buy my suits cheap from him.

I don't really have any negative memories of my childhood, and yet some people might wonder whether my family was somewhat dysfunctional. In her early teens my sister became anorexic and bulimic (though those conditions were not recognized or understood then), and my brother fell sick in his twenties, with symptoms of some neurological illness. He declined to be treated and then one day in August 1997 he disappeared. His body was found a few days later, washed up on the shore beneath the white cliffs of Dover. It was the day Princess Diana died. I was doing a memorial service for her, as I had some members of her family in my congregation, and the police came into the church and told me during the service. I was really upset, though I didn't tell anyone else what had happened until the service was over.

When I was 14, something happened to me that was seriously to affect the next few years. I used to ride a bike – not for pleasure, but to get from A to B – and one evening I fell off it and injured my right knee. This was the beginning of a saga that was to continue into my early twenties, which involved 36 operations on my knee and my groin. Until I was 18 I was in and out of hospital all the time, sometimes for months on end – once for six months – and I can remember being very ill and often in great pain, especially after the surgery. Maybe this is one of the reasons why other people's sufferings are so significant to me now, because I endured so much as a teenager. For years, the district nurse used to come every day to dress my wounds. I had septicaemia three times and each time I came close to dying. The first time I was put into intensive care was on 29 July 1981, when I was 17: it was the day of Prince Charles's wedding to Lady Diana and I recall being very anxious that I would miss seeing it on television.

None of this had any effect on my faith, I have to say. God was always very close to me and I didn't blame him for anything – I just took it in my stride. Nor did it affect my schoolwork. I studied in my hospital bed and often I actually overtook my fellow pupils. When it came to choosing our O-levels, most of us opted to do one that was practical and I put my name down to do child care and development (which one could study at a nearby college). I can recall one of the teachers telling me: 'You don't want to do that. That's a girl's subject!' But I did it all the same and I got an A. As part of the course, I remember, I had to make a dress and a teddy bear.

I was still visiting my elderly friends whenever I could. When I was 16, I was even (to my surprise) chosen by the local council to receive a special 'civic recognition award', which they presented to me at their AGM in the presence of the former prime minister Edward Heath. It was the first time I had ever experienced considerable media interest in me. A year later, I was given the award again – the first person ever to get it twice!

By this time, I was spending all my lunch hours at school with the head of the Sixth Form, a black man called Michael Amos (whose daughter, many years later, was to be Leader of the House of Lords). I used to go through the daily newspapers with him, *The Times* and *The Guardian* and the *Daily Telegraph*, and we would discuss what was going on in the world. He was the most inspirational figure of my youth – and, unlike my teacher when I was ten, he told me that I *would* do anaesthetics *and* would be a priest. (A quarter of a century later, I had the honour to conduct his funeral.)

I was made head boy when I was 16, I suppose because I was very well behaved and very organized, and very much part of the establishment. I was a strict disciplinarian, perhaps under the influence of my father's Calvinism. I had never been one to break the rules and I didn't like other pupils breaking them. If I caught anyone smoking, I used to be so angry! Mr Amos told me once that I was a little dictator, and he wasn't joking.

I suppose that in a sense I seem to have lived my life backwards. My wife, Caroline, tells me that when she first met me, 20 years ago, I was 'certainly not as eccentric' as I am now. Nowadays I am quite jovial, but I never used to be. When I was a child, I wanted only to be with my elderly friends. Now that I am much older, I seem to get most pleasure from being with children. What was the turning-point, if there was one? I have never thought about this before, but maybe it happened while I was at St Thomas', training to be an 'operating department practitioner'. I no longer had the spare time to go and visit the elderly, and instead of being drawn to the geriatric wards I started to specialize in paediatrics – simply because it was much harder than doing adults and I seem to have this strange predilection for things that are really difficult.

Anaesthetic rooms are quite frightening places for children, so I went down to the local shops to look for some suitable pictures to put up on my walls. By chance, I chose several of Paddington Bear (a character I had missed out on myself as a boy, when my mother was reading me *Pilgrim's Progress*). As it happens, my middle initials are PB, for Paul Bartholomew, but my patients soon told me what they really stood for! I had to learn how to stick needles into little children and persuade them that it was fun, and I proved to be rather good at this. After a while, I could actually get them to smile when I said I was going to give them an injection.

There were quite a few who came down for repeated surgical procedures and I got to know them very well and became very close to some of them. I can even remember the name of one little girl who had to come down to the theatre every two weeks to have laryngeal polyps removed. It was very sad. One occasion I have never forgotten was when I was assisting a very good consultant anaesthetist and a little boy died on the operating table. The consultant completely fell to pieces, but I took over and was able to bring the boy back to life. I realized then that even the most skilful practitioner can find children a challenge.

I have taken an interest in them ever since. Maybe I did discover a different side to myself at St Thomas', though I wasn't conscious of it at the time. I have certainly told people since that I only had my youth when I went to theological college, a few years later. For the first time then, I really engaged with people of my own age and enjoyed their company. I remember that we used to go punting at midnight – though I still didn't break any rules. I was also the president of the Cambridge University Eschatological Sausage and Apocalyptic Jelly Baby Society for the Prophylaxis of Depression among Theologians. I remember that some children used to join us, along with all these really eminent academics, as we ate sausages and jelly babies and discussed why there are no cats in the New Testament and how we could get them back in there.

Looking back now, I suppose that my childhood was unusual, and in some ways quite difficult, though I really was not aware of that at the time and I remember it today as a time of joy. I have to admit that I am glad that my sons are not like I was – and yet I hope they will share my concern to help the suffering and repair the broken. In that respect, at least, I am the same person I have always been.

CHAPTER 2

Josiah and Jacob

Josiah is my elder son. He was born in 1996 in St Thomas' Hospital in the heart of London, in a room, overlooking the Houses of Parliament, where I had spent many hours during my training as an operating department practitioner. By this time I was a vicar with a parish in inner London. It did not occur to me for a minute that soon my life would radically change and I would be spending much of my time abroad.

I remember his birth so well. In the lift on the way up to the labour ward we met one of the consultant anaesthetists I used to work with, and as a result Caroline got an epidural immediately with no questions asked. The labour was not easy, but Josiah looked beautiful when he eventually arrived. He was not a placid baby, however. He made a lot of noise every night and, much as I loved him, I was soon wishing I could anaesthetize him! I often walked the streets in the small hours of the night, pushing him in his pram to get him to sleep.

Today, Josiah is much more quiet. He is also sophisticated and exceptionally bright. He goes to a grammar school in a neighbouring county and at the age of 13 is already studying not only French and Latin but also ancient Greek, Chinese and (at home, on his own initiative) Arabic.

He cannot remember a time when I wasn't constantly travelling. He knows that I am often in dangerous places, he knows that even at home the Hampshire police say I am top of their 'at risk' list, and yet he assures me that he is never afraid for me because he knows God is always with me.

Josiah writes:

I like having a well-known dad, because I have met so many interesting people. I've even been to lunch with the Queen. We also had Saddam Hussein's translator come and stay with us. After the Queen, I like it the best when the reporter Rageh Omaar comes to see us.

My dad is often on the news but I don't really like watching him because I've heard everything he has to say before. The times that I really get scared are when they are threatening to kill Dad and he has to get out of Iraq quickly. The last time it happened, we were at Legoland. When we got home, the police came round and made us leave our house. We all prayed for Dad and then we knew he would be all right – I heard God say that to me very clearly. We know that God will always look after him, so I never worry. I do worry about the other children in Iraq. I am also very worried about what will happen when the Americans leave Iraq. I do wonder whether the Iraqi forces are ready to take over, but Dad tells me they have been trained well by the Coalition.

I don't worry when Dad is away a lot because I can always talk to him over the Internet on Skype. I know he is

doing God's work so he has to be away. I know he has a lot
of other children to look after and I am so pleased he can
do this. When some of the children from Baghdad came
over [in 2008], it was so nice. I thought they would be sad
and depressed but they weren't. I actually liked David best
– even though I had never met him before, I knew a lot
about him and he has become my brother. I talk to lots of
the children in Iraq over the Internet and so I really want to
learn to speak their language.

The most important things my dad does are feeding all
the people and trying to find peace. I have been to Israel
and Palestine several times and I really love it there, and
one day when it is safe enough I want to go to Iraq to help
my dad. Once I have been to university, I want to go and
work with him. The religious leaders in Iraq once told Dad
that nobody could take over from him apart from his son,
and one day I would like to do that. I have learned that I
must always help people, and that is what I want to do,
even in very dangerous places. My life is not as important
as saving the lives of other people.

This is my prayer:

*Dear Lord, please look after the people who are not as
privileged as us and can't have the things we take for
granted. Please help all the people like Dad and help all
the people that he helps. Amen.*

My younger son was born in Coventry towards the end of
1998. It was a day I shall never forget, whose extremes of
emotion were a foretaste, in a way, of so much that was to

follow. I had just begun work as a 'residentiary canon' of Coventry Cathedral – the only one in England who was expected to travel a lot! I hadn't yet made even my first trip overseas when I found myself in hospital for five weeks for observation because I had double vision and my balance was going. A few hours before Jacob was born, I was told I had multiple sclerosis.

Jacob came into the darkness that descended on me like a ray of light. He was home before I was and proved to be the perfect baby, always good, always sleeping when he was meant to be, always a bundle of delight. Actually, he was big and ugly at first, but he grew to be one of the most beautiful little boys I have ever seen – though, as the years went by, he also became a bit naughty.

Now he is 11 years old and attending a nearby prep school. He enjoys his academic work but he really lives for sport, and especially rugby. He follows my work closely and talks to me most days. He, too, has visited the Holy Land several times with me, and he has absolutely no fear about what I do. Often if I am home in England for more than a few days he says to me, 'Isn't it time you went back to work now?' I used to tell him that I also had work to do in England, but I don't think he really believed me.

Jacob writes:

It is strange to have an unusual daddy – I meet a lot of people who I would not meet if I had a normal daddy. One of my best friends was Yasser Arafat, who even gave me his *kafiya* [Arabic headscarf] for my birthday and signed it for me. Soon after he gave it to me, he died – I was so sad, I cried. Daddy went to his funeral, so I told him to send some flowers from me. I even used to speak to President Arafat on the phone.

When my daddy is away, I chat to him on Facebook and Skype. I also talk to a lot of my friends in Baghdad and in Charlotte, in America. I don't worry about Daddy because God is always with him.

When some of the Iraqi children came to England, it was as if they lived in hell and had come to heaven. David is different from all the others because he treats me like a brother and I love him. When Daddy is not here, I know he is with David and our other friends in Iraq. When I see him on TV, it is like I am there with him. I always wonder what he is doing every day. I am very fortunate, because my mummy looks after us like a mummy *and* a daddy.

Every day, I pray for our friends in Iraq and the Holy Land, and this is what I say:

Dear Lord Jesus, please be with Daddy wherever he is in the Middle East. Look after him and all our friends in Baghdad and Bethlehem. I especially pray for David and all our other friends in Baghdad – do not let any bombs hurt them! Thank you, Jesus. Amen.

I love being with Josiah and Jacob and I miss them so much when I am away from them. When I come back to my family in rural England, I feel at home as soon as I walk in through the door (though sometimes I do wake up the next day and wonder where I am). As a father, I am not a 'dictator' at all but am rather indulgent. I have to ask Caroline what the rules are and then I have to try to uphold them. Usually, the boys come and ask me for money when they know that she would say no, and then, when I give them some, they promise me: 'We won't tell Mummy.'

I have never thought, even once, that I am 'missing out' on their childhood, or that I need to 'make up for lost time'. I do come home regularly, every three or four weeks, even if it is only for a few days; and whenever I go away again I always make sure I say goodbye to them. Do they miss me when I am away? Recently when Caroline came to Lebanon with me, Jacob insisted on coming as well, because, he said, 'I'm not letting her go out of the country without me.' Josiah often asks me whether I love him as much as the children in Iraq, and lately he actually *told* me: 'You love them more than me.' And that did upset me, a lot. It doesn't make me think that what I am doing is wrong, but only that I need to rebalance the way I treat my own sons, to really make them a priority when I am with them. In church circles today people often talk of the role of fathers, and I know how important it is. As my friend the evangelist J. John often says: 'Children need presence more than presents.' I am acutely aware how little time I spend with my boys and I know that the older they get, the more important it is that I make them feel special. When I am at home, I need to make them and Caroline feel that they are the most important people in my life – which is what they are!

People are always so positive about my work, but there are not so many who appreciate the price my family has to pay to make it possible. I know that without the three of them I could not do it. They enable me, inspire me and release me to do what I have to do in some of the toughest places in the world. They, too, are part of my ministry, and my calling is also theirs.

CHAPTER 3

Children of the Holy Land

I have worked for many years in Israel/Palestine, mostly at a very high level with government ministers, presidents and prime ministers. I have also witnessed the brokenness in the Holy Land (or, as I prefer to call it, the land of the Holy One), where everyone is a victim in a sense, and many of the victims victimize others in turn. I have not spent the amount of time there with children that I have in Iraq, and yet the impact that children have made on me there has been very great. Let me talk about just a few of those with whom I have been deeply involved.

One city where I have spent a lot of time is Bethlehem, which as a 'little town' two thousand years ago saw the birth of the most celebrated child in history: Jesus, the Son of our Living God. Over the years I have become as familiar with the city as if it were my own home town. Since my first visit in the 1980s, I have been there in good times and in bad times – and there have been many of those! I have seen Bethlehem's streets ploughed up by Israeli armour; I have seen the massive concrete wall being built, 26 feet high, that today hems in its houses and leaves its population no room for 'natural growth'. I know many of the families that live there, who have suffered in so many ways. Children suffer especially in times of conflict, and over a third of Bethlehem's inhabitants are under 15.

Most of the people that I and my colleagues from Coventry Cathedral helped there were Christians, but not all by any means. For example, we supported a clinic based in a mosque in a nearby village. It served over two thousand people, including all the local children, and it had a wonderful garden and a playground. Then several enormous wire fences were built through them both and obliterated them. The local children cannot comprehend that this was done to protect the people of Israel – all they know is that the people beyond the wall wanted to deprive them of their playground. Today they live in fear of 'the other'.

The principal community I have worked with in Bethlehem is the Syrian Orthodox. Many of their ancestors were living in Palestine long even before the birth of Jesus. Others fled there from southern Turkey during the First World War, when so many of their people were massacred, along with the Armenians, by the troops of the Ottoman Empire. (Others, of course, ended up in what is now Iraq, and later I was to discover that many of my friends in Bethlehem have relatives in my congregation in Baghdad. Today I often find myself conveying messages between them!)

One member of the Syrian Orthodox community to whom I became particularly close was a carpenter called Yusif, who made tourist souvenirs out of olive wood. He used to keep me informed about what was really happening in Bethlehem, and in particular he would tell me of the needs of its children. He had three lovely children himself: a girl named Despina, then Jacob and then a little girl called Lara. I knew all three of them well – I had known them since the day they were born and had seen them baptized – and I truly loved them.

When Despina was little, she developed serious spinal problems and it was clear that she needed major surgery. None of the hospitals in the West Bank had the necessary equipment or expertise, but there was a surgeon in Israel who could do it if we could find the thousands of dollars it would cost. In those days I was still working at the International Centre for Reconciliation in Coventry and we did not have enough money to pay for the long and complex operation; but my friend Patrick Sookhdeo came to the rescue and his Barnabas Fund made up the shortfall. The surgery was very successful, though several follow-up operations were needed, and Despina was sure that God was with her. Slowly she recovered, and she proved to be a most exceptional girl. She did very well at school and is now, aged 17, at Bethlehem University, training to be a nurse.

Yusif made me a wonderful gift – a chair fashioned out of pomegranate, orange and lemon wood and decorated with silver and mother of pearl. I couldn't take it with me out of the West Bank – it is as large as the throne I sat on some years later in Saddam Hussein's palace in Baghdad! – so today it has pride of place on my former colleague Hanna Ishaq's balcony in Jerusalem.

One day when I was with Yusif, I asked him what his community in Bethlehem really needed. His answer was immediate: what they needed and *wanted* more than anything was their own school. Once again Dr Sookhdeo came to our assistance, providing the funds to buy and extend the building that is now home to the finest school in the whole of the West Bank, where today the most wonderful children are receiving an outstanding education. It sounds so straightforward, but it was not. I remember standing on the roof one day while the Mar Ephraim School was still being built – and being shot at, presumably because I was regarded as an intruder. I remember the terrible day when our brilliant young architect, Ghassan, was killed. Everything seemed to be going wrong, but we persevered for the sake of the children.

In fact, it was soon after Despina's surgery, in 2002, that everything *really* went wrong. I and my colleagues from Coventry had been working so hard for peace when the Israelis launched a military operation they called Defensive Shield to try to suppress the increasing violence of the Second Intifada (or 'Uprising'). It was not long before the Church of the Nativity in Bethlehem was under siege, after more than 200 Palestinians – a mixture of heavily armed gunmen, policemen and civilians – took refuge there when the Israeli Defence Forces invaded the city in search of wanted militants. I was involved in the negotiations to end the siege[2] but I was equally concerned to ensure that the people of Bethlehem could eat, after the IDF imposed a round-the-clock curfew on the city that was lifted for only a few hours every four days.

I was still allowed to move around, and so Hanna and I would load our car with food and take it to people's houses. When we went to Yusif's one day, his children told us that now they knew for certain that we were angels. They had had no food and had been praying that they would get

2   I have told the full story in Chapter 2 of *The Vicar of Baghdad* (Monarch Books, 2009).

some – and then we had arrived! I assured them that we were not angels, and insisted that if anyone was, it was them. Those days were so dark and dreadful. I didn't know how I could keep going, but I would escape to the children and they, without knowing it, would encourage me and give me strength.

Despina writes:

My grandfather grew up in Jerusalem but in 1960 he and my grandmother and my aunt were forced out of their home and made refugees. We still have the key and the deed for the house, but someone else is living there now, so we can't go back. My grandfather brought his family to live in Bethlehem. They had no money and there were no jobs, so they sold my grandmother's jewellery and bought a shop and my grandfather started a business making and repairing shoes. When my father was young, the family was very poor and there were many days when they had nothing to eat, not even bread.

My father and one of my two uncles carve things out of olive wood for the tourists to buy. When I was little, the whole family was involved in this work and we had plenty of money. Today, we are very lucky that my mother has a job at Bethlehem University, because several years ago the tourists stopped coming.

Up until 2000, our life was good. We had freedom to move around and I can remember how we would drive to Jerusalem and the Galilee in our own car and see many beautiful things. Now I can't leave Bethlehem without a permit. Only at Christmas and Easter can I get a permit to go to Jerusalem, and only because my family is Christian – but I don't like to go there now anyway because all my happiness is stolen from me when I have to go through the wall and the checkpoints. My country has always had war, and every one of my family was born in wartime. One of my cousins died during the First Intifada, in 1989, when he was 13. He was in the street when people were throwing stones at the soldiers and he was shot in the heart.

When I was six years old, doctors discovered that my spine was not growing straight. I had to wear an iron brace around my body all the time, and it was so uncomfortable and heavy and made it difficult to sleep. When I was nine, they inserted some metal in my back to make it straight. Without this, I would have died very quickly, because the curving of my spine was crushing my lungs. The operation, which took almost 12 hours, cost $24,000. My family had only $500, but Father Andrew helped us to find the money.

This was at the beginning of the Second Intifada and Bethlehem was put under curfew. No one was allowed to leave their house. After the operation, my wound became infected and the doctors said I had to have antibiotics intravenously three times a day at a local hospital. The streets were full of Israeli soldiers and I remember that once they surrounded our car and pointed their guns at my father and me. It was a long time before they let us go to the hospital, even though my father had a letter from the doctor and I had the IV cannula in my hand. On other occasions they shot at our car and I remember my father trying to shield me from the bullets. It is a miracle we were never hit.

The worst time in my life was during the siege of the Church of the Nativity. We had watched as Yasser Arafat was surrounded in Ramallah, live on TV, and had seen many, many people being killed there by the IDF. They said they were going to invade the whole of the West Bank to find terrorists. We were so afraid! Early the next morning, their tanks arrived on the streets of Bethlehem. The noise was horrible and I felt dreadful when I saw them. Our road was only narrow but more than a hundred armoured vehicles forced their way down it, damaging the buildings and destroying many cars. The tanks were so big we could see the tops of them going past our second-floor window. The men who were afraid the soldiers would seize them hid in the Church of the Nativity – they thought they would be safe there because it's a holy place. The tanks and soldiers surrounded the church for 40 days, and since we lived in the next street we were surrounded, too. We couldn't even go out onto the balcony of our house.

When the curfew was first imposed, I was happy because I didn't have to go to school. We had experienced curfews many times and we expected this one to last just a few days. We never imagined it would go on for 40 days. We were trapped in our house. The water pipes and electricity lines had been crushed by the tanks, so we couldn't cook food or watch TV and there was nothing to do. It was winter, so it was very cold. I was ten years old, my brother was eight and my sister was just a baby. I had to sleep on the floor in the passageway, because my bedroom was next to the street and if a shell from a tank had hit the house the front wall would not have been enough to protect me. The food we had lasted only three days and after that we had nothing. We were so hungry! Our neighbours had some flour and they made some bread and tried to throw it to us from their balcony, but it fell down into the street, where an armoured vehicle drove over it. However, one day a soldier found out that my sister was only a baby and he gave her his own food. The first word she ever spoke was 'tank'.

Father Andrew was the only person who could help us. Somehow, on our tenth day without food, he came to our house with a big box of supplies. There were even nuts. It was a miracle. My father gave half of the food to our neighbours, even though we didn't know how long the curfew would last, because they had many children and they were hungry, too. The siege went on for another 27 days. We were living with nothing – in fact, I think we were not even really living. It was horrible. The soldiers destroyed so much of Bethlehem and they even blew up my grandfather's little shop. When he saw it, he cried and cried.

Two years ago, we had to move after our house was wrecked by Israeli soldiers for the fourth time. This time, they had come in looking for men who were fighting them and they broke everything, even the toilet. We are not terrorists but we are never really safe. I'm not scared when I see the soldiers, though I don't know why; but I am scared when I think what could happen to people I love.

The children of Bethlehem are very diverse, but their needs are very real. Despina is not the only one who has required medical attention. There is Yusif, with diabetes, whose insulin we have been getting for him ever since I first met him; and then there is Shadi, with cystic fibrosis, whose medical expenses we have paid for years. Sadly, like the children in Baghdad, many of them do not have fathers in work and so their families' incomes are very limited. At Christmas, we buy toys for all these children in an attempt to give something back to Bethlehem in gratitude for what Bethlehem once gave us.

My work in the Holy Land has not been just in the Palestinian territories but also in Israel, where it has been very high-profile. I would often spend weeks at a time there, meeting politicians. I saw very few young people, but there was one, a girl called Roni Shavit whom I have known since she was very little. I remember well holding her hand at her brother's funeral in Jerusalem many years ago. Most of all, though, I remember her talent. With Roni, it wasn't anything she said that gave me hope, it was her exceptional playing of the piano. She is by far the finest musician, of any age, I have ever met. When things in Jerusalem got especially bad and I felt that I needed spiritual direction, I would escape to her house and there I would just listen to her play. Today, I have a recording of her playing on my mobile phone and I listen to that when things are especially bad in Baghdad. She helps me in a very different way from the others, but her help is very real.

Roni writes:

I met Andrew, so I am told, when I was about one year old, when he was bringing groups of clergy to Israel as part of

his efforts to achieve reconciliation between the Israelis
and the Palestinians. My father was the tour operator,
so he invited Andrew to our home and a special bond
formed between us all. Andrew has been a member of our
mishpacha (family) ever since, and he never misses a chance
to visit us.

Today, I am almost 18 and studying piano at the
Jerusalem Academy of Music. I think the first time Andrew
listened to me playing was when I was a seven-year-old
beginner, and it was very flattering to see how much he
enjoyed it. Since then, I have met him on his visits to Israel
even when he is here just for one day in his pursuit of
reconciliation. I believe he is trying to get the Israelis and
the Palestinians to understand that the only solution is to
live together in peace. I admire his courage and his persist-
ence, especially in recent years in Iraq. He really believes in
his way, despite the many obstacles and the crazy people in
this part of the world. His faith is stronger than the sad
reality.

I remember when Israel was under terrorist attack
during the *intifada*, just a few years ago. Suicide bombers
were blowing themselves up on buses, on the streets and
in restaurants and shops. It was very frightening for me
and my family, as it was for almost everyone, especially in
Jerusalem, which suffered most. My brothers and I were
not allowed to ride on buses – my parents drove us to
school or to our friends' houses. At that time, Andrew was
visiting Israel very frequently and I believe that his meetings with Israeli and Palestinian leaders probably helped to
dampen down the fire.

My strong hope is that soon we will be able to call Israel a peaceful country, where all its citizens live together in serenity without fear or terror. I believe that Andrew's work is opening the way.

CHAPTER 4

The Street Children of Baghdad

When I went back to Iraq soon after the end of the war in 2003, it was both a wonderful and a sad experience. So much had changed, and so much had been destroyed. There were now a lot of children on the streets, and many were actually living there. Most of them were boys, though there were a few girls. I talked to them all and listened to their stories, though some were quite unbelievable and I could never be sure they were true. Some said they had lost their parents in the war. Others had already been living in orphanages when it began, but these homes had been destroyed or looted and the staff had fled. Some had taken to the streets simply because they preferred the freedom it gave them, as well as the opportunity to meet foreigners. Many of them had become drug addicts or habitual glue-sniffers, which worried me greatly.

In the days before the Green Zone was established, I was based at the heavily fortified Palestine Hotel in the centre of Baghdad. It was the safest place to be – though a number of journalists had been killed there already. Amongst the many children who lived on the surrounding streets were three boys called Laith, Ahmed and Muhammad, who quickly became my friends. Each morning they would be waiting for me in the hotel lobby, and soon a little ritual developed. They would take my bags and then outside the hotel they would polish my shoes, and then they would accompany me to the area outside the secure zone and stay with me until I got into my car. They would spend much of the rest of the day looking for people whose shoes needed cleaning, but in the evening they would be outside the hotel again, waiting for my return.

Once, I asked these boys if they knew my name. 'Of course,' they said. 'It's *Baba*' (which is Arabic for 'Daddy'). When I showed some photos of them to Josiah and Jacob, they wanted to know when they'd be moving in to live with us. How I wished that they could have, but I knew that the best I could do was to help them find food and a proper home in their own city. They had previously been living mainly on US Army rations given to them by the soldiers, but a tradition was soon established that I would take them out to eat with me in a rather run-down local restaurant. In time, more and more of the children joined us. For many of them, these were some of the best meals they had ever had.

In the end, most of the street boys were placed in a home by one of the Shia seminaries. I don't know what became of the girls. Most of them had been raped, and some of them had become pregnant. Ahmed I never saw again, and in 2005 Laith and Muhammad were both killed by a suicide car bomb. When I heard the news I was devastated – it felt as if I had lost my own sons. Someone in the American administration once said of the deaths of maybe half a million Iraqi children as a result of the sanctions in the 1990s, 'We think the price is worth it.' All I can say is that for me the death of children is the most unbearable aspect of violent conflict. Whether or not their names are known, whether or not their bodies are identified, each one is a little human being. This poem by an American peace activist puts it so well:

The Children of Iraq Have Names
by David Krieger, 1 November 2002

The children of Iraq have names.
They are not the nameless ones.

The children of Iraq have faces.
They are not the faceless ones.

The children of Iraq do not wear Saddam's face.
They each have their own face.

The children of Iraq have names.
They are not all called Saddam Hussein.

The children of Iraq have hearts.
They are not the heartless ones.

The children of Iraq have dreams.
They are not the dreamless ones.

The children of Iraq have hearts that pound.
They are not meant to be statistics of war.

The children of Iraq have smiles.
They are not the sullen ones.

The children of Iraq have twinkling eyes.
They are quick and lively with their laughter.

The children of Iraq have hopes.
They are not the hopeless ones.

The children of Iraq have fears.
They are not the fearless ones.

The children of Iraq have names.
Their names are not collateral damage.

What do you call the children of Iraq?
Call them Omar, Mohamed, Fahad.

Call them Marwa and Tiba.
Call them by their names.

But never call them statistics of war.
Never call them collateral damage.

The only child I met on the streets who was a Christian was David. I first saw him sleeping in the back of an American Bradley fighting vehicle. He was only 12. The American soldiers liked him, and within a month he had learned the basics of English from them and after three he was fluent – and speaking with an American accent. I took him with me to the opening of St George's Church. Immediately after the war the congregation had consisted of diplomats and soldiers, but within weeks it had become too dangerous for foreigners to worship outside the Green Zone and the church then became increasingly Iraqi and numbers grew rapidly. When I was not in the country, the services were taken by my wonderful colleague Colonel Frank Wismer, the American Episcopalian who was the senior chaplain to the Coalition Provisional Authority. David really looked up

to him. Here was somebody who was a Christian *and* in
the army – the two things he liked most!

He quickly became very close to me and every day when
I left the Palestine Hotel he would be waiting for me in the
lobby, to polish my shoes and carry my bags. Whenever I
was in Iraq – which now was often – he was constantly at
my side. He would always eat with me, and would tell me
stories of all he had suffered – although at least one of them,
that his father had been murdered by Saddam, turned out
to be a lie. He was clearly enjoying life now, and he had no
sense of fear. He would go everywhere with me and my colleagues. It wasn't long before he was calling me 'Daddy'.

I will never forget the day I was with the Chaldean
Catholic patriarch, Immanuel III Deli, and suddenly he and
David started talking to each other in fluent Aramaic. I
asked David how he knew this language and he told me it
was what he had spoken at home – it is what all Iraqi Christians speak. I knew a little Aramaic from my time with the
Syrian Orthodox community in Jerusalem and Bethlehem,
but this was the first time I had heard it used in everyday
conversation. I had assumed it was a dead tongue used only
in liturgy. David still spent a lot of time with the American
soldiers, and since many of them were Hispanic it didn't
take long for him to learn Spanish as well. So, now he could
speak Kurdish, Aramaic, Arabic, English and Spanish. Not
bad for someone who had just turned 13.

Like most young teenagers, David could be very difficult.
However, by now he really did see me as not just his friend
but his father, and I regarded him as a son and loved him as
one; and so he was always with me, come what may. When
eventually the time came for me and my colleagues to move

out of our hotel into the large and beautiful house that was to become the Iraqi Centre for Dialogue, Reconciliation and Peace, it went without saying that David would move in with us. For him, it was like going to heaven. Never before had he lived in such a house, with a garden and a swimming pool and a view of the river.

It was at this time that I realized how important he had become to me. Eighteen months had now passed since the end of the war and most of the time we were working on various crises. David could tell when things were going badly and he would come over to me and say: 'Shall we talk to Jesus about it?' We did, and things were always better. The house was in a Shia area next to the Tigris, about seven miles from the Green Zone, so every day we had to commute into the centre of Baghdad for meetings with our contacts in the Coalition. David couldn't come in to these, but he would stay in the car with our security men and he told me he always prayed for us. I'm sure he did: he may not have known what we were doing but he knew that we needed God.

The house became known as 'the Centre' and it received many visitors, from politicians to religious leaders to British and American diplomats. All of them got to know David well and whenever anyone asked him who he was, he would say simply that he was my son. It often struck me that through him I had learned what it is to be a child of the Almighty. I had found him and I had always loved him and always forgiven him when he did something wrong, and in return he loved me. In the same way, I had been found by God and had always known myself to be loved and forgiven by him, and I loved him in return. David was teaching me things about the grace of God I never learned at theological college.

Amidst all our work with Iraq's religious and political leaders and amidst all the hostage negotiations, there was David. I tried so hard to get him to school but it was so difficult. Classes were intermittent, as the teachers were often unable to get in – and indeed some were kidnapped or even killed. I often wondered whether anyone ever thought about the effect of the conflict on the children. Time and again, I would think of those words of Jesus, in the KJV: 'Suffer the little children to come unto me.' In Iraq, no one was 'suffering' the little children – but they were certainly making them suffer! For a year David went to school when he could, but, with 80 children in his class and constant disruption, he often came home in a far worse state mentally than he had gone. At the age of 14, he decided he was not going any more. There was nothing we could do to change his mind. He was naturally so clever, but school was impoverishing his life, not enriching it. I gave up fighting with him and allowed him to stay with us. He spent his day travelling around with us and swimming.

David tells everyone he has saved my life three times. One night in 2004, at about 11, I was sitting at my computer when suddenly I heard him shouting for me from the garden: 'Daddy, Daddy, come quickly!' I ran out and there he was, standing over three young men who were lying face-down on the ground with their hands tied behind their backs. David had an iron rod in one hand and their identity cards in the other. At first, all I could think was: How on earth did he get them down? When I asked him, he said simply that he'd copied what the American soldiers did.

Our security men soon arrived on the scene and we learned that the three men were opportunists who had been hoping to rob us.

The second occasion was when a minor figure in Saddam's regime was brought in to the Centre in the belief that he was actually someone else who was one of Iraq's most wanted men. His captors knew we had close links with the Coalition and Iraq's interim government and they wanted us to turn him in. I informed the Americans that we had a suspect, and three hours later (having got lost on the way) a very discreet group of men from the special forces arrived to take him away. By now, the news was all over Iraqi TV that the vice-chair of Saddam's Revolutionary Command Council had been caught. Forty-five minutes later, David suddenly announced that the house was being surrounded by plain-clothes police. One of our security men bundled us up onto the roof, and when I looked over the edge it seemed as if the whole of the Ministry of Interior was outside. I shouted down to them that we no longer had the suspect, but the only response was that some of them rushed up onto the roof and pointed their guns at me.

David was not going to stand for this. Without hesitation, he jumped in front of me – no one was going to shoot his daddy. He shouted at the policemen to lower their guns, but they clubbed him so hard around the head that he fell unconscious – and then they started hitting me. After a few minutes, David regained consciousness; he was a little crazy and tried to attack the policemen and we had to hold him back. Eventually they all left, taking with them over $20,000 in cash and equipment. This incident was so serious that it was even discussed in the House of Commons

two days later (though it was David that I was most concerned about). The upshot was that the British ambassador
insisted that I should move back into the Green Zone,
which I did.

The third occasion when David says he saved my life was
when he pleaded with me not to accompany Iraq's National
Security Adviser, Mowaffak al-Rubaie, on an important
visit he was making to meet the leaders of a Shia mosque
near al-Khadamiya. For some reason David had a bad
feeling about this, and very reluctantly I agreed not to go.
In the event, there was an attempt to assassinate Dr Mowaffak; some of his bodyguards were killed, and he himself was
wounded in the arm. If I had been there, I would certainly
have been a target too.

For the next four years, I had to live in a little trailer in
the Green Zone when I was in Baghdad. Meanwhile, David
went to live in the St George's compound. I would still see
him two or three times a week – and every day, wherever I
was in the world, I would phone him (and if I failed to do
so for any reason, I was in big trouble). Eventually, once he
had reached the age of 16, he would often come and stay
with me in my trailer, where he would do all my chores.
When he was old enough to start a proper job, I found him
employment at the church. At first he did some general
cleaning, but after a while he joined the staff of our new
clinic as assistant to the dentists, who all told me he did a
very good job. To tell the truth, he wouldn't have fitted in
anywhere else in Iraq.

It was in 2006 that I discovered that his father was still
alive and living in Kurdistan. When I asked David why he
had lied to me, he told me that he had 'nothing to do with

him'. Like many Iraqi men, his father had no real interest in or concern for his children, and David had not had any kind of relationship with him. Eventually, I was able to make contact with him and we discovered that he is very ill. My Foundation has supported him ever since.

In 2008, along with five other young people from St George's, David accompanied me to England for a month. I thought it was very important that congregations that had supported the church in Baghdad so faithfully should not just hear about the people of St George's but should actually have a chance to meet some of them. I couldn't get visas for any adults to come to Britain, but I was able to get half-a-dozen children into the country. This was not without complications, however. In Baghdad, we had to wait two days for a plane. Our scheduled flight to Amman never arrived, so we flew to Istanbul instead and on to London from there. We lost all our luggage, and some of us never got it back – but we did make it to England eventually and they all had the time of their lives. They even had lunch at the Oxfordshire home of the British ambassador to Iraq, and they also spent a couple of days at the House of Lords. David was delighted that so many people knew of him already from my books or from articles or TV documentaries about me. All of the children were greeted like stars wherever they went, but especially him.

In the early summer of 2009 I moved out of the Green Zone back to St George's and it was agreed that whenever I was in Iraq, David would be with me all the time. And so he is. To be honest, I could not do my work without him.

David writes:

From the beginning I have always gone to church, but the priests never spoke to us and they were always very boring. One day, I was near the tank where I used to sleep amongst the American soldiers and the other children around me said to me, 'You're a Christian; go and talk to that man over there, he's a Christian priest.' I said: 'I don't want to see a priest.' But then he came over to me. I called out to his assistant, 'I am a Christian. I want to brush your shoes,' and this priest let me.

Then, he invited me to come to the opening of his church the next day. I spoke to the American captain, Marvin, before I went and he said, 'Make sure you come back!' That first service was full of soldiers and diplomats – the church was surrounded by tanks and there were helicopters flying overhead. It was very strange: I thought there were Christians only in Iraq.

When I saw this man's love, I said to him, 'Will you be my daddy?' and from that day onwards he has been. I love him and he loves me. Since then he has always been with me, in good times and bad. I have saved his life three times. When he was sent out of the country [in July 2007] because people were trying to kill him, I cried on the phone to him. He told his assistant Samir to take me to Jordan to see him, and when I did I cried and hugged him for an hour. When Daddy came back to the church, it was more than lovely. So many people started to come! We used to have hundreds but now we have thousands and St George's has the biggest congregation in Iraq.

I haven't always been very good and I've made mistakes,

but I've always loved my God and I've always loved his people. The American soldiers used to be like a family to me. They didn't trust Iraqis at first and so they were always asking me who was good. One day, an army chaplain prayed with me. He said I was 'a smart child' and told me that Jesus would look after me. I thank my God because he sent me my daddy Andrew and it has changed my whole life. When I first went to England and met Josiah and Jacob for the first time, it was wonderful. I had always talked to them on the phone and we knew that the three of us were brothers.

Throughout the conflict and many difficulties, my God has never left me since I was a small boy. He talks to me and I talk to him. One day, he even sent an angel to me. At first I was scared, but then I heard a voice saying to me: 'Don't be frightened, David! You will be all right. Your angels are with you.' Then the angel left and I called Daddy in England – it was 2am his time. Then I went into the church and prayed for an hour and worshipped God because he had sent me a message.

From that day on I have loved myself, my God, my people and my enemies, as Daddy has always taught me. Every day, I ask the Lord Jesus to protect me and my country, to protect my church and to protect my adopted family: my daddy, my mum Caroline, Josiah and Jacob. I pray that our Lord will also protect all the American military in Iraq, and that they will all be filled with the love of Jesus. I pray that I will always do what God wants me to do. One day, I know I will be a preacher like Daddy and will tell everyone what God has done for me and how he can do the same for others – and he will.

CHAPTER 5

The Children of St George's

Recently, I sat down with some of the children of St George's and we talked about the past few years. Most of them had no recollection of life without conflict. Some of them spoke of the days when their families fled the fighting in Baghdad. Others told how they had had to stay indoors 24 hours a day to avoid the bombs and rockets. Then we spoke about the many problems since the war ended. One of the mothers present began to cry – the pain was just too much. For the children, though, there was no thought of how awful it was. All they could talk of was how wonderful church was and how much they loved Jesus.

At every service, we have a slot where people can tell us about what has happened to them over the past week. They talk of how they have seen God working, of how they have been saved from death; but then there are also always stories of the injury, kidnap, torture or murder of loved ones in Iraq's unending trauma. The children are never far from these incidents. I look at these dear young people and once again I am challenged. They know what is going on and yet they are always mindful of the good and forget the bad. How different it is for adults! The pain their mothers feel is intense. They see the needs of their children – not only for food and water and medicine but also for education – and it hurts them, and so they cry and plead.

These children do not have regular school. Sometimes their teacher has been killed or kidnapped and has not been replaced. Sometimes they are in classes with over a hundred other children. They have all witnessed the suffering and distress of their families. They have all known what it is like to go hungry. They have all had times without clean water, in a city where temperatures can reach 50°C in the shade. Some of them live in terrible conditions, without proper homes, under roofs made of corrugated plastic that let in cascades of water when it rains. And yet they are all clean and immaculately dressed. They never complain or ask for anything, and for all of them coming to church is always a highlight of the week. The problem is getting them to go home afterwards!

I would not want to suggest that Iraqi children are somehow more angelic than British or American ones, still less that they are better brought up. If anything, I suspect that their culture is generally less kind to children than our Western cultures are. Also, in time I have come to realize that the children at St George's are on their best behaviour when *Abuna* is present, because they see me as a representative of God – which I suppose demonstrates the high regard they have for the church and its priests. They may very well be much naughtier when I am not around. I also have to acknowledge that, though all of the children of St George's have seen, and in some cases suffered, terrible things such as very few children in Britain and America have seen or suffered, they are aware that everyone around them is experiencing the same things. I do think that makes a difference.

It would also be wrong to imply that all the bereaved children I have met in Iraq have such a positive view of life. For those who have lost both father and mother the outlook is very different and their reactions are usually more extreme. My experience of this is much more limited, because all the children we have had at St George's who have been orphaned were soon moved away out of the capital, generally to live with relatives in the north (although some have gone abroad, some even to Australia). At least they have the support of the church community. Three orphans I do know well are Muslims, whose uncle now looks after them in Jordan. Their parents were doctors and were shot dead in 2005 as they left their hospital in Baghdad. The eldest of the three, Zaid, was 11 years old at the time. At night, he used to sit in his bedroom and bring out his most treasured possessions: the handkerchief, still covered in blood, that his father had with him when he was killed, the watch his father was wearing and his mother's mobile phone. He would hold them tightly and say nothing. Four years on, when I last saw him, he still could not talk about his parents' murder, though his whole life and all his thoughts seemed to revolve around what had happened to them. When his uncle Ali asked him whether he wanted to be a doctor like them, his answer was clear and emphatic: 'What's the point? All that studying, just to get killed!'

I am used to bad days – to terrible days, even; but 22 June 2009 was the worst I had known for a long time. I had been working on the case of the five British hostages taken in Baghdad more than two years previously. What was different about this case was that four of the men were my friends (indeed, often my bodyguards) and I had lived alongside them. This day, we learned that two of them, both called Jason, had been killed. When I heard this news, I confess I cried. I had hoped and genuinely believed that we would get these men back. Young David was with me and he cried, too, simply to see me in pain.

It was a Sunday and I heard the news as I was preparing for our main service at St George's. For a while, I felt I would not be able to lead it – but then the children arrived. That day, we were going to look at the biblical story of David and Goliath: little Alan was going to play David and I (at six foot three) was going to be Goliath. So, I knew I had to be there. We acted out the story and I fell to the ground on cue and the children came over and pretended to chop off my head; and then they sang and processed back to Sunday school. As I looked around the church at the many hundreds of people in my congregation, I realized that I could not see one person there who had not suffered too.

As we reflected on the story of David and Goliath, it was a vivid reminder that the seemingly small and insignificant people of God can overcome a mighty evil. After the service and the long, long process of saying goodbye to the congregation that followed, I went back to my room and there I found a group of the children waiting for me. They knew I was sad that day and they wanted to cheer me up, so they sang to me and told me how much they loved me. To me, it was like David and Goliath – I felt so small and weak in the face of all I had to deal with, but God was giving me the strength I needed. In the evening, I was preparing for my departure for Oman the following day when a call came in from Breanna, one of the young people in Charlotte. She, too, had heard the bad news. David said: 'Daddy, see, Breanna is the first person who has made you smile today.' And it was true.

Once again, I saw how in the hardest times it is often only the children who give me real hope. They know now that they can make a difference, because without them I would not be able to keep going through what at times is like hell. With them, I know I can do all things through Christ who strengthens me. Once again, I had learned from the children. Once again, I had seen things through their eyes, not adult eyes, and once again I was aware of the presence of the Almighty. As we say each week at the Communion, '*Allah hu ma'na wa Ruh al-Qudus ma'na aithan*' ('God is here. His Holy Spirit is here'). For us, these words are not just part of the liturgy, they are true in every way. I will never forget what a famous preacher said to me once. I was talking with my friend Rodney Howard-Browne, the head of Revival Ministries International, about the need for preachers to be dynamic, and he remarked that the problem was that so many had 'not seen God'. Then he said to me: 'You have seen him, though. You've seen him in the children.' I suddenly realized that he was right. I have indeed seen God in them, and that is why they are so important to me.

Some of the children of St George's have formed an inner circle. These are the children at the church who are closest to me and they decide who is in the circle and who is not – I have no say in this. They have made up their own rules, which are very strict, far stricter than any I would ever impose. It is this inner circle that used to meet me from my armour-plated car when I arrived at the church for a service. They stay with me and look after me, providing everything I need. They come into my study, or wait outside it. They only ever call me 'Daddy', never '*Abuna*'. I tell them that I love everybody in the church – and I do – but the fact is that this group of children are like my nearest and dearest. When some of them came to England with me for the summer in 2008, one of the girls, Fulla, became very close to my younger son, Jacob. I said to them: 'When you grow up, you should marry each other.' She couldn't stop laughing at that. 'I can't marry my brother,' she told me. 'We have the same daddy!'

When I ask the inner circle what they do for me, this is what they say: 'We take care of you, we love you and feed you, give you your medicine and do church and business work. We tell you about the Iraqi people and their life and culture. We tell you what you need to know about Iraq.' In reality, the most important thing they do is love me. I have given each of the older ones a mobile phone and I ring them all regularly (and if I don't, I'm in trouble!). Our conversations are brief and simple: they tell me what they have been doing, I tell them what I have been doing and then we tell each other that we love each other and that's it. Increasingly, we also try to tell each other what we expect of each other – but, to tell the truth, they require very little of me except to love and love and love, not only them but other children, too, especially the children in Iraq. They see me not just as their priest but as a kind of superfather. Of course, I am not a super father and never

1. A curious child – though, at five years old, evidently none too interested in the elephant at London Zoo.

2. On the children's ward at St Thomas' Hospital on Christmas Day, 1986. At the age of 22, I still look uncomfortable holding a little child.

3. Back on a bike, at Clare College, Cambridge, during the invasion of Iraq.

4. Josiah and Jacob in 2009.

5. Poor street boys in Baghdad, next to two of the thousands of brand new, armour-plated cars the Coalition and its contractors have brought to the city.

6. Little Vivian, much as I first saw her, kneeling in prayer at the front of the church.

7. One of the street boys, cleaning my size-16 shoes.

8. With Laith, Ahmed and Muhammad. The satellite phones they are playing with were rare and valuable objects in 2003!

9. David.

10. Havan holding a calendar made with her drawings.

11. Johnson.

12. Despina in Bethlehem.

13. Using two 14-year-old girls, called Mariam and Amira, to show the people of St George's how old Mary probably was when she had Jesus.

14. Roni at home on her piano in Jerusalem.

15. Out with the inner circle in Baghdad. On my right is Lena, my PA in Iraq.

16. Fulla, Lina, Mabel and one of the Sandys.

17. Hanging out in Charlotte with a former colleague, Jason, and five of my American 'inner circle': left to right, Anna, Destiny, Micaiah, Emily and Sophia.

18. Lost in thought with a lollipop with most of the inner circle at St George's.

19. With Micaiah in Charlotte. When I first met her, she was a little girl; now she tells me what to do.

20. Children from St George's mixing with some of my congregation from the Coalition chapel in the Green Zone.

21–3. Not your usual Christmas. In the middle photo, I am playing one of the wise men.

24. Angelina.

have been. I feel guilty about being away from my own sons so much.

These children remind me of the verse in 1 Corinthians 13 that says that love 'always trusts, always hopes, always perseveres'. If I had to sum up my relationship with all the children at St George's, if I had to summarize what they have written for this book, I would simply quote those words. Despite all they have endured, they always trust, hope and persevere. That is their very nature. It is this that I think children seem to practise better than adults. There is total continuity in their love. There may be violence all around, they may have suffered, but they do not give in. They don't even know what it means to give in.

Consider how these children express these three aspects of love. Love 'always trusts'. It's very easy to imagine that amidst such suffering trust would soon disappear. These children place their trust ultimately in God. As Johnson says below: 'The soldiers [protect] themselves with guns but I [protect] myself with prayers.' The children know that God is always with them. Everyone else may give up, but not God. The older ones say they always trust because God has given them so much. These are people who have almost nothing! I ask them, 'What have you been given?' and they all give the same answer: what they have been given, here in Iraq, is Abraham, Daniel, Jonah and Mar Thoma (St Thomas). To them, in other words, what is so important is the patriarchs and prophets of the Old Testament and the one miserable apostle, Doubting Thomas. They may have very few material possessions, but they all know of their spiritual heritage and it's in this that they place their trust. As far as they are concerned, this is what inspires trust in them. They trust with total certainty. This is what children have to teach us.

The second aspect is hope. For them, their hope arises out of their simple belief in God, who they say has never left them and has never left Iraq. It was interesting to see how surprised they were to discover that many of the Americans who came to their country were Christians. They knew that *they* were; they knew there was a future for them in heaven and in a simple way that was their understanding of the Kingdom of God – that one day they would be with Jesus and it was he who would care for them. They really believe that the Kingdom of God belongs to them: God has given it to them, they have no doubt that it's theirs. To be honest, they see God as a wise and good dictator – everything that Saddam Hussein was not. At school, they used to have to sing about their 'king' from Tikrit (Saddam's birthplace), how great he was and how he had everything under his control; but they have always trusted absolutely that the One who is really in control is God. Their certain hope has always been that he will look after them and one day will take them to be with him in heaven.

This brings us to the third aspect of love: perseverance. There is no doubt that these children will keep going. I ask them why they will never give up and they tell me that one day they will be next to Jesus on his throne. What is more, they insist, they will not be on the *left* of his throne, as I have told them they will be, but on the *right*. They will sing in Aramaic, which happens to be Jesus' language as well as theirs, and so he will understand what they're singing. I assure them that Jesus will understand all languages, but here in Iraq nobody doubts for a moment that their language is the one Jesus speaks.

It is this love of theirs that enables me to overcome all my fears. We are told in 1 John 4.18 (in the NKJV): 'There is no fear in love; but perfect love casts out fear, because fear involves torment. But he who fears has not been made perfect in love.' This love that always trusts, always hopes and always perseveres must indeed be perfect love, because I have no fear. However difficult and dangerous things get for me, I think of these children and their love and I am not afraid. They really are the ones who keep me going, who enable me to do what I have to do. I often describe my day in Arabic terms as *yom asal* or *yom basal*: a 'honey day' or an 'onion day'. In Baghdad there are lots of onion days, when everything seems to go wrong, when people you love are injured or killed, when the good news you've been given turns out to be a lie; and yet you have to keep going. What is it that enables you to do so? For me, it is the children, young and innocent.

One of the members of my congregation who was actually brought to faith by all his suffering is a boy called (strangely) Johnson. As it happens, he is David's best friend, though for some reason he doesn't qualify to be admitted to the inner circle. He was only ten when the war broke out in 2003, and his story is worse than terrible. He has had two of his favourite uncles killed, one of them right next to him, and he himself has twice been left for dead. His family of ten now live together in a single room since their home was blown up in 2004. They live on the food they are given by the church. Their only income is the $30 or so a month Johnson earns for painting houses and the $50 a month his brother usually gets for installing a couple of satellite dishes. Johnson himself has nothing – and yet he knows he has everything because he has Jesus.

His earliest memories of the years of conflict are of going without food for four days, because his mother had none to give him. That is why the war was so terrible, he says, even though it was short: because there was nothing to eat. He recalls collapsing from hunger and being taken for dead, until a woman passing by realized that he was still alive and tended him until he was conscious enough to eat something. This woman saved his life. Johnson has always longed to see her again but never has. He says that maybe she was an angel. Maybe she was.

One day towards the end of the war, he went with his mother to see his brother on the other side of the river. After waiting for seven hours to cross a bridge, they saw an American soldier who, on learning that they were Christians, let them through. That was when Johnson really discovered what war entails. Around the checkpoint on the bridge, there were some 70 bodies, some lying on their own and others piled up in heaps. Most of these people had been killed by air strikes. For two days after that, Johnson could not sleep. The bodies were buried in a common grave, but dogs came and started to dig them up and eat them. All he could think of was that when he died he, too, would be eaten by dogs. He couldn't find any of his friends, and the whole area smelt of decomposing corpses.

When the huge statue of Saddam was pulled down in al-Ferdos ('Paradise') Square, Johnson was scared just to think what the dictator would do to the people responsible. Even as a ten-year-old he knew that Saddam had killed many people. Then everyone started looting the presidential palaces, filling their cars and even lorries with the things they had stolen. The Americans fired rubber bullets at the looters but that didn't really stop them – they just went to another palace and broke into that one. After that, they burnt all the palaces down. It was all so awful. This is Johnson's memory of the war and the chaos that followed it.

To this day, he is surprised that so many people turned to violence once Saddam had been removed. Indeed, for Johnson the real war was not the bombing and the invasion by the Coalition forces but what happened afterwards. He expected that things would get better, but in fact they got worse. He recalls: 'The soldiers were protecting themselves with guns but I was protecting myself with prayers. All day and night I could hear the bombs. I thought this was the end of Iraq.' He used to go fishing in the Tigris, but he had to stop because there were so many dead bodies floating down the river. Some of the things he saw are simply too dreadful to repeat.

In 2007, he went to the animal market with his brother James and one of his uncles to sell some birds. (For Johnson, this was the nearest thing to going to a zoo. There are no dogs or cats at the market – Iraqis don't like them – but there are many other different animals, including hundreds of birds dyed yellow and pink and red with food dye.) His uncle had recently got married and hoped to make some money to set up his new home. He and Johnson had just sold six birds and were going to buy some clothes when suddenly there was a huge explosion. Johnson can remember his coat being on fire and taking it off – but after that, nothing. When his brother came looking for him, he found his unconscious body placed among the dead but fortunately he saw he was still breathing. Their uncle had not been so lucky.

Johnson did not regain consciousness for four-and-a-half hours, and he was badly injured, and yet he was kept in hospital for only a day. Another three days passed before he learned that the bomb had killed his uncle. When he first heard the news he did not react at all, but in the night he got up and broke every window in the house. This man had been not just his uncle but his best friend. It was a while before Johnson's family managed to stop him doing more damage to his home and to himself.

His mother had been a member of the congregation of St George's ever since she was told to come by her next-door neighbour, a woman who is not even a Christian but a Mandean (a follower of John the Baptist) who comes to the church every week and even works in our clinic. The lay leaders of St George's began to go regularly to pray for Johnson, and he says now that he immediately felt much better. They taught him how to pray himself, and they became his friends. As soon as he was able to, he started coming to the church himself, even while he was still on crutches.

There are very few people at St George's who have stories to tell of coming to faith – most of them have always loved Jesus. Johnson is one of the exceptions. The atrocity he experienced has driven him to the Lord and his Church, and now he finds great strength in his faith. Over two years later, he is still an active member of our congregation. It isn't easy for him. Although his extended family are actually

Christians, Johnson's paternal grandfather married a woman who was a Muslim and had to embrace Islam himself in order to do so. As a result, Johnson, too, is identified in his papers as a Muslim – and in Iraq once a Muslim means always a Muslim. Nonetheless, he will not give up. To him, he says, going to church is like eating: you have to do it simply to stay alive. After all he has been through, he can testify that God loves him and protects him and will always do so. Despite all his sufferings and the scars they have left, his church and his faith fill him with hope for the future.

One of the young people at St George's comes from a family not of Christians but of Mandeans, an ancient religious community that has been very badly persecuted over the last 20 years in Iraq, where their numbers have fallen from over 60,000 to fewer than 5,000. Havan is very serious about her love for Jesus. Her great gift is her ability to draw and paint – and, unlike most Iraqi children, she does not merely copy existing pictures but creates her own. Still only 15 years of age, she is able to express what she has heard and seen in images that convey very powerfully both the pain she has witnessed and the hope she feels. I am constantly amazed at how much she manages to communicate.

Several of her drawings and paintings are reproduced in this book. In her picture of the children coming to Jesus, you can see how much they have all suffered. But then there is her picture of a little boy planting a flower on the path. I can see that Havan has taken in what I have so often said, that the job of a peacemaker is (as my late friend and co-worker Sheikh Talal Sidr once put it) 'pulling up thorns and planting flowers' – and that the children themselves are my hope for the future of Iraq.

CHAPTER 6

The Inner Circle, in their Own Words

It is the 21 children of my inner circle in Baghdad, above all, who keep me going. Their names are Alan, Angelina, Bashir, David, Fulla, Kristin, Lina, Mabel, Maher, Mardina, Mariam and Mariam, Martin, Mona, Nahrain, Sally, Sandra, Sandy and Sandy, Stephani and Yusif. (There is now also one more, Micaiah, as I shall explain later.) They are the reason that I, too, trust, hope and persevere. I love them all and I will never forget them. Here are some of their stories, told mostly in their own words.

Fulla writes:

When I was nine years of age, we lived in a run-down neighbourhood of Baghdad – me and two sisters and one brother and my parents. I would hear a lot of talk about a coming war with the United States of America and other countries. All I knew about this war was that it was something horribly scary and that if it happened we would leave Baghdad.

I used to hear stories from my schoolmates about the loved ones they had lost in earlier wars our homeland had gone through. The countdown continued, until on 8/9 April 2003 we woke up to a terrifying cacophony of explosions and dreadful sounds I had never heard before. My parents tried to keep us calm and quiet, though I could clearly see the terror and confusion in their eyes. The next day we left for Mosul, to live with relatives in the north until the war was over – they said that other provinces were not being targeted like Baghdad.

It was a very difficult time as we shared bread and water. Then, one day, we heard on the radio that the regime had been toppled. They said there would be no more dictatorship but a new situation where poor people would be able to eat and drink well and justice would be done.

When we returned to Baghdad, we were surprised to see how many houses had been destroyed. Our own home was no longer habitable, and so the first problem that faced us was to find somewhere to live. I could feel the travail my parents were going through. Luckily, my father's friend was leaving Iraq and so we were able to live in his house. We had no school, so we spent most of the time playing or listening to religious programmes on the radio. Then our money began to run out. My father could not buy us toys, or even meet our most basic needs. He had always been not just a father but a kind, good friend – he worked as a driver for the Red Cross, which suited his character well as he loved to help other people – but now his behaviour began to change and he didn't seem to be the same person at all.

After a year, we had been robbed, our house had been burnt and now my father was ill, having suffered a stroke from worry and exhaustion. We were now living in my grandparents' house to save money, as my mother's work was our only means of support. My father's illness kept him in bed for two months and six days. I wept whenever I looked at him – his struggles with sickness and death seemed never-ending. I prayed to the Lord that he would get well. My mother, too, was always praying and going off to the church to perform special prayer rituals. Soon my father could stand on his feet, not as steady as before but much better than we had dared to hope.

In the meantime we had moved into an empty apartment, whose owners had fled the country in fear of their lives. Fortunately, my aunt's family lived nearby, as well as some other old friends, and the church was close, too, thank God! There were some nice people in the congregation who helped us, and we received many gifts from people both in and outside Iraq.

We learned a lot about the Bible, and from the Gospels we learned what is right and what is wrong. I learned how to regulate my life and how to order my relationships with my friends. I was even more glad when I met Father Andrew – he was so kind and considerate, and enveloped me with a warmth that only my father had shown me before. He soon succeeded in bringing happiness into our home as he proved to us that what we read in the Gospels is true: the Lord can help us to overcome the trials and difficulties we face through life. Nowadays when I visit my relatives and friends, I feel that I am indeed fortunate, because so many of them are in need of a father like Father Andrew, who can make their lives seem better and brighter. I can only express my thanks to God for all the good things he has brought me and my family, and call on everyone to take the road of Christian faith, so that happiness and love will enter their hearts, too.

Lina writes:

I am the eldest of four children in my family. When the war started in 2003, I was only ten years of age. Things in Baghdad were worse than terrible – bombs were falling all the time. It became so dangerous for us all that my father decided we should seek refuge in my grandfather's house. This was still in Baghdad but it had a basement, and there we all lived underground while the fighting continued. My parents had had good jobs as civil servants, but when the war started they both lost their jobs and their salaries and it wasn't long before our family was really suffering. We had nothing – all we could do was pray continually that our most merciful God would protect us and help us. We lost everything, including our home, and yet we didn't lose heart but thanked God for everything, and especially each other.

At the end of the war, my family returned to al-Dora [one of the main Christian neighbourhoods of Baghdad], but my father did not want me to stay there [because so many Christian girls were being raped and killed by the militias] and so I moved into my aunt's apartment in Haifa Street, which was near to a good school. It was also very close to the Anglican church of Mar Gorgis – St George – which had been closed before the war but had just been reopened. We started going there and found that it was a

holy and wonderful place. Six years later, I am still a
member of that congregation. I go several times every
week, to give as well as to receive. The people there are so
kind and tender-hearted! They are true Christians, full of
love, mercy and humility. We are like one big family.

I have also become very close to our amazing priest,
Abuna Andrew. He is so full of the love of God! He loves
everybody, of any faith or background. I love him so much
and so do all the people in the church, because he helps us
all. He has helped my family and even gave my father a job
at the church, which was wonderful. In 2008, I travelled to
England with five of my friends from St George's to stay
with *Abuna* Andrew and his family. We went to many
different churches and prayed and sang in them. We don't
call him '*Abuna*' now, we call him 'Daddy', because he is
not just a priest to us, he is like our daddy. He does everything for us and cares for us all. When my father wanted
me to get engaged, Daddy said that I couldn't because I
was only 14 and he told my father so. I was so happy!

So, I have lived in a very violent place but I am not afraid,
because God has allowed me to be a member of a wonderful church family and has given me a daddy who loves and
cares for me. My family may have lost everything, our home
and all our possessions, but I have not lost the people I love.
I pray each day that God will keep us and all people safe. I
wish that everyone would follow Jesus and find faith in him,
because he is always faithful to us.

Kristin writes:

I am one of the students of the Sunday school at St
George's. I was born in 1997 in al-Mansur in Baghdad, in a
convent where my father worked as a guard and my
mother was a domestic help. At the end of 2002, my family
moved to al-Dora. My father had a job working for a very
important man in the government, looking after his farm,
and we repaired an old house there and lived in that.
However, ten days after the war started, the farm and the
house were hit by an American bomb. We escaped to the
north, to the town of Karkush, near the city of Mosul.
When we came back to Baghdad after the war, we found
that the house in al-Dora had been totally destroyed and
our furniture had been stolen, so we had to rent a flat.

My father got a new job with a contractor making the
concrete barriers that the Americans were putting everywhere in Baghdad, but then, in September 2004, he was
kidnapped by the terrorist group al-Tawhid wa'al-Jihad
['Unity and Struggle']. They tortured him badly and forced
him to pray with Muslims; otherwise, they said, they would
kill him – which they said they were allowed to do, because
he was a Christian. We were praying all the time and God
answered our prayers and they released him, along with
some others, for a ransom. We went back to Karkush and
borrowed some money to rent somewhere to live; but
after two months we came back to Baghdad again so that
my sister and I could go to school. Everything in the city
was so expensive and so difficult! We rented the second
floor of my grandmother's house. My father started
looking for work, but to this day he hasn't been able to

find any. My brother, Yusif, is six years old now but he can't speak or see. We have taken him to a lot of doctors, but none of them has been able to do anything for him. We have only our Lord Jesus and Father Andrew. We pray and we pray, and I ask everybody who reads my story please to pray for us too. In spite of all our hardships, I am very good at my studies and I have now finished primary school.

We were invited to St George's two years ago for the first communion of one of our relatives. When I saw the church, I just loved it. Ever since, I have gone every Saturday and Sunday. My sister and I both celebrated our first communion at St George's. I love the services and I have made new friends there – and then when I met Father Andrew he gave me the gift of hope. I love him so much. I love his prayers and the way he loves us all, and especially that he loves all of us children so much. We pray that our Lord will keep him in good health and keep him at this church, because he loves us and we love him and we need him so much. Amen.

Mardina writes:

I live with my mother and father and my three brothers in Karada Mariam, just outside the Green Zone in Baghdad. I am at home all the time now, I don't go to school any longer. My family would worry if I went because I'm a teenage girl, and I'm scared to go there in case I'm killed by a bomb or kidnapped.

When the war broke out, we escaped to the north to the village of al-Hamdaniya, where my grandfather has a house. When the war was over, my father went back to Baghdad to see what the situation was, and in particular to see the state of our neighbourhood and our beautiful house. There was no electricity and no water and none of the infrastructure needed for a normal life. What is more, my father had lost his job in the presidential office looking after visitors to Iraq.

He sold his plot of land and bought us a little house to live in in al-Dora so that we no longer had to pay rent (which makes a big difference) – but then the sectarian violence forced us out. We had to leave our house and all our new furniture and run away with nothing but the clothes we were wearing.

After six months, we asked one of our old neighbours what it was like in al-Dora now and he said that the neighbourhood had been destroyed. The terrorists had taken everything in our house: all the furniture, the doors – even the wiring. My father went and told the police but nobody listened and we couldn't get any compensation from the government. We still haven't been able to go back, after all these years. My father used to get an emergency payment of 80,000 dinar [about £40] a month from the government, but since 2006 he has received nothing, because the people who administered the funds fled to another country, taking the money with them.

Sally writes:

I live in Baghdad in the area called al-Alawi. I was born in 1989 and grew up in my grandfather's house with my father and mother, my sister and my two brothers. We were a happy family and my parents worked very hard to give us a good and stable life. I was very happy at school with my friends, and I studied very hard. In the holidays, we all used to go to the park – none of us felt any fear. I also went to the Mother of Sorrows Church every Sunday, to pray and to build up my faith in God and Jesus and the Bible and to learn from Father Nadhir what we should do to help others. I was a member of its youth committee.

Since the war, our life has changed. Now it's a struggle, all uphill. So many bombs and rockets had hit our neighbourhood that it was no longer the same place. We escaped to the north, to my grandfather's house in Karkush, where we hoped to find safety and freedom from fear. We stayed there for two months, but for me it was a very difficult time because I was away from my school, my friends and my home. The future was dark and we had no idea what would happen to us. We didn't have any money and my father and mother had to look everywhere to find something for us to eat. We were very dependent on the support of our friends and relatives there.

When we returned to Baghdad, we found the city in a very bad state. It was like a graveyard. Some of my friends had fled abroad, and I missed them. My father couldn't find a job; my mother started working as a tailor, to earn enough money for us to live, but that affected her health and she became weak, though I tried to help her as much as I could. After a while my father found a badly paid job in a shop that sold alcohol, but he had to give it up after a few months because the terrorists tried so many times to kill him. A man who worked with him at the shop was injured. My sister and I had to leave school and stay at home all the time. Then the militias took over the area; they attacked our house and terrorized us and tried to expel us from our home and make us leave. All we could do was trust in God. We kept going to the church, but it closed after it was hit by a rocket (though God protected the church and the rocket didn't explode).

Then, one day, we went to St George's to attend my cousin's first communion. When I entered the building, I felt something beautiful fill my heart, as if there were angels around me. I wanted to be a member of that beautiful church and I started to go there four days a week. On Thursdays, we pray for sick people and for people who have been kidnapped and we ask for peace in Iraq. On Fridays, there is choir practice. On Saturdays, there is the Mothers' Union service, and on Sundays there is the normal service for everybody.

After a while I met Father Andrew, the spiritual father of the church. He is like a gift from heaven: his heart has room for everyone and he helps everyone. We are his children, and I love to call him 'Father'. We pray that God will keep him and protect him. Amen.

One day, Father Andrew said he wanted to take me to Britain with some of my friends from St George's. My parents agreed to let me go and Father Andrew organized the trip, and also paid for it. Those 28 days in 2008 were the most beautiful days of my life. Father Andrew's staff worked very hard so that we could have a wonderful time. We travelled all over England and visited lots of churches and met lots of kind people who prayed for us and promised to support us. When we visited one church, I shared a room with the daughter of the priest there; she was very kind and now I feel she is like my sister. We also met Father Andrew's family: his beautiful wife, who welcomed us like a mother, and his two boys. We loved them all and will never forget them.

Mariam Bassam is a dear girl whose father was a key member of our security team at St George's until one day he was killed in a multiple terrorist attack. The church continued to support his family but they had to move back to Nineva in the north. Still, they always come back to Baghdad for their holidays. Mariam's best friend was her cousin Vivian, the little girl who died of cancer of the bladder in 2007, and so she has lost two of the people she loved the most. In spite of all she has been through, however, she is full of the love of Jesus. And even though she is usually far away from Baghdad, she is still a vital member of my inner circle.

Mariam writes:

I am just a little girl from Baghdad. I used to have a wonderful, happy family – my dad, my mum, my brother, David, and my sister, Anissa. My father worked at St George's as a guard, until one day four years ago we heard he had been killed. I was eight years old at the time and my dad was very important to me, and suddenly I could not play with him any more or call to him. I was so sad and desperate, because I had lost my dad for ever. I had lost his face and his voice, I'd lost his presence in my life.

We moved north to live with my grandparents in the town of Karkush, as we couldn't afford to live in Baghdad any more. I could no longer go to my school in Baghdad; I could no longer go to St George's all the time to see my wonderful Father Andrew, who has always looked after me and my family and provided anything we needed. When I come back to the church, I always imagine my father standing at the gate doing his duty and protecting the church and the people inside it, like he used to. I see my friends playing with their fathers, or going out to the zoo or the amusement park with them, and I just want him to come back to me.

I miss my friends at St George's and at my school in Baghdad. I like being with them, playing and studying with them. I am waiting for the day when we can come back to live in Baghdad, the city that I love, where I was born. I pray that God will bless my Father Andrew and keep him in good health and heal him. I pray that my church will keep growing – it is already the biggest church I have ever seen. I pray that God will make me something in the future so I can help my family. Amen.

Yusif has been coming to St George's for many years, since soon after the church reopened in 2003. Like many of the children born after the Gulf War of 1991, he has serious deformities and he is confined to a wheelchair. Of all the children of St George's, he is one of the closest to me, and he is also one of the few who are always at the church. He comes with his mother – his father is no longer alive and he has no brothers or sisters. It's difficult for him to get into the church or its offices – he is not light and it isn't easy to carry him in – and so he usually visits only one or the other each day. He has a very important role at St George's: every Saturday and Sunday we give $100 to a different member of the congregation, not because they have earned it in any way but simply as a wonderful sign of the love and grace of God, and this is Yusif's responsibility. Up and down the aisle he goes in his wheelchair and he chooses one person, young or old, male or female, to whom he gives the money that will transform the week ahead for them. He has never made a mistake and given it to the same person twice.

Yusif writes:

I was born in September 1999, in a small house with only one bedroom, a bathroom and a small corridor which serves as a kitchen. My mother had a very difficult pregnancy, but it was when I was born that the problems really started. I was seriously disabled, not least in my legs, which won't grow. I saw a lot of doctors and had many operations and I hoped I would be able to walk, but I never have done.

When I was three years old, my mother registered me at a church kindergarten which my best friends went to. There was a bus to take me there and bring me home, and the headmaster was very nice to me and used to carry me from and to the bus. They taught me drawing, the Arabic and English letters, mathematics, prayers and singing to the Lord. I used to get through a lot of trousers because I was playing on the floor all day.

During the war, we escaped to our relatives' house in al-Karada, because they have a basement where we could hide from the bombs and rockets. I was scared, but my mother would say: 'Come on, let's pray! The Lord will keep us.' After a week we went back to our home and my father said: 'We will not leave this house again. If God wants us to live, we will live; and if God wants us to die, we will die.'

One morning, after the war was over, we were having breakfast when we heard the sound of gunfire. The noise came closer and closer and my mother said, 'Let's go and hide in the bathroom!' (because there are no windows in that room). There was shooting and explosions for one-and-a-half hours, and when we came out of the bathroom we saw that all the glass in the windows had been broken. Many houses had been destroyed and all the neighbours were crying with fear.

After I graduated from the church kindergarten, I joined a special school for handicapped children but it is a long way from my home in al-Zafaraniya, so we have to get a taxi there and back, which is very expensive. I cost my family too much – they had to pay for eight operations for me from when I was six months old until I was five – and so for four years I went only twice a week. I passed my first year with honours and have been top of my class ever since. Now I am in the fifth year and I have to be there every day.

In my second year, my dad was ill for eight months or so and then he was in a coma for a week. My mother said to me, 'If you love your father, pray for him!' but he died in

May 2007 and my mother became my mother, my father and everything for me. Since then, she has dedicated herself to me even more than before, because I am all she has left in this life. We still live in the house I was born in and I don't want to move. This house is everything to me: my father was here, all my memories are here, my happiness is here.

I have been very lonely sometimes, but since we started coming to St George's Church I have found some lovely friends. Now I spend most of my days at St George's and I feel that everyone cares about me and loves me, and I love them. I can see that my mother has changed, and her view of life: she was desperately sad after the loss of my father, but now she isn't thinking so much about the past because she serves the church and spends most of the day there with me and everyone else there.

I would like to thank Father Andrew for his help. I love him so much, from the bottom of my heart, and I am always praying for him and ask God to give him health and peace for ever. Despite all my difficulties, I thank God for everything. Amen.

CHAPTER 7

Dancing in Heaven

There are some children who cannot tell their stories because they have already gone to heaven. I want to tell you about two in particular: Aziz, a boy of five, and his 15-year-old sister, Ranin. Their father, a man called Raad Azo who had lost a leg as a soldier in the Iran–Iraq war in the eighties, owned a little kiosk on the street. In 2004, he came to me with two photographs I shall never forget. They were pictures of these two children lying on a table, dead. They had just been to church and were wearing new clothes – they were so loved by their family! Aziz had been selling ice with his father just before he was killed.

They had been shot through the head because their father sold alcohol. The militiamen had wanted Raad to leave the country and had threatened him, but he wasn't able to. After the murders, we, too, tried to get him out of Iraq with his remaining family – his three other children were then aged 13, 11 and nine – but without success. The family had stayed in their house in Baghdad throughout the war, though the children were terrified of the American planes, and now they say they will never leave. Today, they are all active members of St George's. Raad was one of the first Iraqis to join the congregation in 2003 and I still see him most days. He carries the photos of his two murdered children with him everywhere, though they are really too terrible to show anyone.

There are so many other children like Aziz and Ranin who have suffered so much but cannot speak for themselves. We remember them all – and we know they are in heaven, singing to their Lord Jesus in Aramaic.

One other child I must mention. I have already told Vivian's story elsewhere, in *Iraq: Searching for Hope*[3] and *The Vicar of Baghdad*, but I have to include her here, as she was one of the loveliest and bravest children I have ever known, and one of the dearest to me. I first noticed her in my congregation at St George's soon after the end of the war. My eyes were drawn to a little girl sitting near the front with her family. She didn't have any hair and it was obvious to me that she had been having chemotherapy. After the service, I talked to her parents and learned that she was six years old and had a very rare form of cancer of the bladder.

Each Sunday during the communion, she would come up to the front of the church and kneel with her hands together. Although she was obviously very ill, I could see that she was full of joy. After the service, she would play happily with her cousin and best friend, Mariam, and I would often go over and give them both a kiss and they would sit on my knee and we would play together for a while before I had to go and deal with the grown-ups. Vivian never complained to me about her illness. In spite of all the suffering she faced, she was still thankful to God

---

3   Continuum, 2005, 2007.

for everything he had done for her and she never had any doubt that he would make her better. I often saw her praying fervently, asking him for a miracle. I remember thinking that she was living proof that God really did design each one of us individually and make us beautiful.

Then, one day, her father told me the hospital had said that her cancer was growing and there was nothing more they could do for her. I took Vivian in my arms and prayed simply that we would find the right person to treat her. I didn't know what else to pray. I was acutely aware that I was asking for something almost impossible. The very next day, after chapel in Saddam's old palace, I met a major I had never seen before who turned out to be 'just a urologist' at the US Army combat support hospital. Not only that, but it transpired that he specialized in the very type of cancer that Vivian had! He arranged for her to undergo surgery to remove her bladder in the King Hussein Cancer Hospital in Amman, and in the space of a week I and the supporters of my Foundation managed to raise the tens of thousands of dollars needed to pay for it.

Whenever I passed through Amman on my way to or from Baghdad, I would go and spend time with Vivian. She would sit on my knee just as she used to in church and I would stroke her hands and she would stroke mine. At first, only her father was with her in Jordan and so she would always want news of her mother and brother and sister, and especially her cousin Mariam. I couldn't tell her that Mariam's father had just been killed. Eventually, the time came for her to have her bladder removed. I remember getting down on my knees to pray for her safety. A former colleague of mine, Fadel Alfatlawi, was by then looking after her and her family in Jordan, and I was so relieved when he rang me to say that the surgery was done and seemed to have been successful and Vivian was back on the children's ward.

Despite the extensive chemo- and radiotherapy she had to undergo, she was soon back on her feet, running around and dancing and enjoying life. I remember going to visit her on my way back from Iraq to England, and it was so good to see her happy, though in pain. I saw her a little later, after she was discharged from hospital to be with her family again, and she was playing more energetically than I had ever seen her play before.

However, seven months later, when I was in Baghdad, I was told over the phone that the cancer had reappeared, in her left eye. A Cat scan soon confirmed that she now had secondary cancer. We did not give up hope, but it was not long before she began to deteriorate. She started to feel ill, she could no longer see very much and her dancing ceased. Now she spent her days lying on a settee. Still, she was very happy whenever I turned up with Fadel. One day, he told her that when she was older he would marry her. She said that she couldn't possibly marry him because she was going to marry *Abuna*.

Whenever I saw her, I would pray with her and it was clear that she had no doubt that God was with her. As her condition continued to get worse, she would tell us about the angels she could see and we would say we were looking at them too, though actually we could see nothing. What was obvious was that she was approaching heaven and its doors were opening wide. She talked about it more and more and we knew for certain that that was where she was going.

I was actually packing to fly to America for a conference on healing when Fadel phoned, early in the morning, with the news that my dear little Vivian had died. In her last hours she had asked when Jesus was going to come and take her to heaven and when *Abuna* Andrew would come and help her.

I don't think I have ever cried as much as I cried then. I had the assurance that she would now rest in peace and rise in glory, but that did not diminish the immense pain I felt. In fact, as the hours went by, it only got worse. Her funeral the next day was the most difficult I have ever conducted. I have buried my father, my brother and my grandparents and taken the funerals of many children, but none of them was as hard as that of little Vivian. I put on her wrist a bracelet that the children of Charlotte had made for me, which was one of my most precious possessions. I read some of the messages that had been sent by the hundreds of people all around the world – Christians, Muslims and Jews – who had fallen in love with her, though they had never met her, and had been faithfully praying for her. (Even Donald Rumsfeld had sent a lovely message.) I preached on Jesus' words of comfort to his disciples at the beginning of John 14 – 'In my Father's house are many rooms. . . . I am the way and the truth and the life. . . .' – and I closed with some prayers that Jim O'Beirne, the head of the Office of White House Liaison at the Pentagon, had written specially.

I have learned to cope with the deaths of adults, even of those who are close to me – and I have lost a lot of them. Children, however, are a totally different matter. I have not learned to cope with the death of a child. It hurts me so much. In human terms, the principal reason for Vivian's death was that Iraq was broken, and that included its health service. It seems likely, too, that the very unusual tumour she developed was a result of the bombing of her country in the Gulf War nine years before she was even born. The depleted uranium used in a lot of Western munitions is notoriously carcinogenic and Iraq is full of its dust. Vivian's suffering was of a piece with the suffering of all the children of Iraq after nearly 20 years of sanctions, war and chaos.

Still, God could have saved her. We had had such hopes for her, we had prayed such prayers for her – and so many had been answered; but then we had lost her. This little girl whom I loved so much was no longer with us. Why was I not angry? I remember saying at her funeral that she was now in heaven, where she was needed more than on earth, and I actually do believe this. I cannot be angry about this – least of all with God. I have never been angry with God. I do believe in miraculous healing and I have seen many people healed, and yet for me it is always only a remission. Complete healing comes only in death, when we are reunited with our Maker, as I believe Vivian has been.

I have said before that I have a very simple, childlike faith in God. Like my people in Baghdad, I love him and do not doubt him. We see so much trauma and tragedy all the time, and God is all we have to hold on to. His love is all that sustains us. There is much I do not pretend to understand but I know for sure that our Lord is with us in the midst of all our suffering. Maybe this is why I am so close to children. I have never seen them angry with God about the things they see all the time. I am not one of those Christians who claim to have all the answers. Some of my conservative friends find it easy to blame every evil on the Fall. For me, all such certainty is a delusion. There are so many questions we will never know the answers to until we get to heaven. There is only one thing I am really sure of: 'Jesus loves me. This I know, for the Bible tells me so.'

Was our praying all in vain? Some of my friends in Charlotte sent me some words from a song sung by the American country singer Martina McBride, called 'Anyway', which expressed my own feelings: that, even if all our dreams and prayers and labours may well come to nothing, we should go on dreaming, praying and labouring all the same.

I will never forget little Vivian, and even now I miss her every day.

1. The Virgin of Iraq

2. Jesus sweating blood in Gethsemane

3. Suffering the little children . . .

4. Terrorists attacking a school

5. Bomb damage, with St George's in the background

6. The Crucifixion

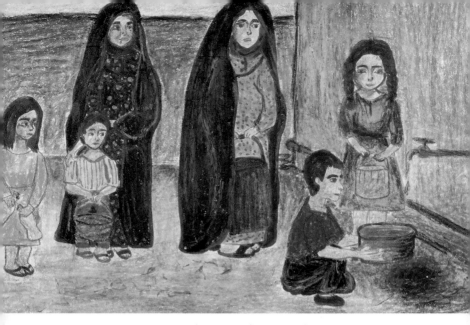

7. Fetching water from a standpipe

8. American soldiers on patrol

9. Planting a flower of peace

10. The Ascension

CHAPTER 8

The Children of Charlotte

So far I have written mainly about children in war zones, but there is one group of children who live in peace and security who are just as important to me. These are the young people of All Nations Church in Charlotte, North Carolina. For several years I have been going to this church that Mahesh and Bonnie Chavda pastor. It isn't Anglican or Episcopalian and yet in many ways I have come to regard it as my spiritual home when I am not in Baghdad – and once again it is the children there that inspire me and keep me going. Wherever I am in the world, they will be in contact with me, by e-mail, text or phone or via Facebook or Skype. They are like family to me and I love them too.

They talk not only to me but also to the children in Baghdad, whom they chat to on the phone or over the Internet. They know them all and have made each one of them a bracelet which has either 'FRIENDS' or the child's name and mine written on it. In fact, they have made these bracelets not only for the several hundred children of St George's but also for all the adults. These simple gifts have become a symbol of belonging to the church and everyone wears them all the time. In April 2009, some of the American soldiers in Baghdad asked the children of St George's what they would like as a present – they told them they could have anything – and they all said: 'Bracelets!' They had to be exactly like the ones the young people in Charlotte had made for them, so we just had to place a new order!

The children of All Nations may live in safety far from Iraq but they are always with me. I look at the bracelet I am wearing now and it says

Abuna loves JEN MAJS RN DSJ GWD and B

which stands for 'Josiah, Emily and Nathanael, Micaiah, Anna, Jacob and Samuel, Rebecca and Nicholas, Destiny, Sophia and Judah, Gloria, Willie and David and Breanna'. These children are the American equivalent of my inner circle in Baghdad and whenever I am in Charlotte we all meet together in a house in Diamond Drive, Pineville. My own sons have been to Charlotte and spent time with them. We may all live thousands of miles apart from each other but we are one family. Whatever happens to any one of us, everybody else knows.

It is so good that all these young people span the divide between war and peace: it shows that children in normal places such as America can also play a vital role in the task of peacemaking by praying and giving support. In Christ we can be truly one – and modern technology can actually help us in this. Thanks to the wonders of Skype we have even been able to link up during services, so that in Charlotte and Baghdad we have been together. We have even had singing competitions between the children over the Internet!

(St George's always wins, but then we do have more children.)

All Nations Church is very Pentecostal, and the e-mails I receive from the people there can be very powerful. Here is a typical one that arrived one day in February 2006. It was written by three of my young friends at the church, who were aged between 12 and 15 at the time.

Dear Andrew,

We just had an incredible night! It started out as a normal sleepover, watching movies and such. Then we began to talk about the youth of today, and today's church, when all of a sudden we all got this feeling that we needed to pray. We felt like we needed to pray for President Bush, for protection! We prayed for many different countries. It was weird but we saw many bombs being planted, and where they were being planted. One of the key places was in the Taj Mahal. When we saw this image, it was a cloudy day and a lot of people were standing around. The other location was at the Super Bowl, we saw Condoleezza Rice watching the game, then after the National Anthem some jets flew over and bombs went off. We prayed for the protection of all who were there, and that the bombs be thwarted.

We realized that Shadrach, Meshach and Abed-Nego needed each other during prayer. We felt like there was a battle. Actually, we not only felt it, we saw parts of it. During our time praying, we saw different angels around us. We even saw a couple of demons, which we cast out of our house. Through all of this, we felt God's presence in the midst. He was with us the entire time. We prayed for you. Emily had a vision of you, then saw complete darkness [and] then there was blood. We felt like He wanted you to know more than ever that He is covering you with His blood. Brett saw, when she was praying for you, that God was healing you as we prayed for you . . . so, be HEALED!

This was the most amazing, astounding, incredible night we have ever experienced! I hope that you have been blessed. We will continue to pray that the Lord will protect you and all of your staff! HEALING IN THE NAME OF JESUS!!!

Much blessings, love and hugs from

Brett, Alyssa and Emily

This was my response:

My dear friends Brett, Emily and Alyssa,

It is midnight here in England and I have been in deep prayer for the three of you. You remember rightly that I prophesied to you many months ago that you were Shadrach, Meshach and Abed-Nego.[4] I have been praying about this. Remember when they were in the flames, King Nebuchadnezzar came to see why they were not burning

---

4 The biblical story of Shadrach, Meshach and Abednego and the fiery furnace is told in Daniel 3. It is set, of course, in what is now Iraq.

and he saw not three in the furnace but four. The fourth was the Son of God. And God is saying that the Son of God is with the three of you. Last night he was with you. He will stay with you, though at times when he is with you it will not be as intense as last night and at other times it will be even more intense.

Remember that the message of the three was to the King. Your message will also be to the rulers of the world. It will begin by me taking it to them sometimes, not all the time; I will give you knowledge of the very difficult things I need wisdom on. You will pray to God and he will answer you; you will tell me what he says and I will tell the leaders the word of the Lord. God will tell me when I am to bring these things to you. You will ask the Lord and he will speak to you. You three have been set aside for a very, very special task. This is a mighty, mighty move of God. As you are listening to him, you will be blessed like you never could have imagined. You will challenge the church and speak God's word to them. I think you should tell the pastors about this; learn from them and love them and show your love to them, because this is partly what God is calling you to do: Love.

I love you so much, my dear, dear friends. I also think God is going to equally use Josiah and Nathanael. God has his hand on them, too, and will use them. I love you all.

Blessings, my friends.

Andrew

My relationship with these children is totally different from the one I have with the children in Baghdad. They live in safety, surrounded by love and care, and have no reason to fear destruction, trauma and death. They call me 'Andrew', because to them I am just a friend. But they are very important to me as well. Like the children of St George's, I believe that they give me more than I give them.

There are three families in particular: the Deckers, the Norbys and the Lanes. They are all very close to each other – two of them live in the same road – and they spend a lot of time together. They all have in common both a great depth of spirituality and a great sense of fun, and the parents all play an active role in the leadership of All Nations. Most of the children have biblical names. And then there is Breanna, a 15-year-old from another family whom all the children in St George's love and every day they ask me when they are going to speak to her next. That isn't easy, because there is an eight-hour time difference between Charlotte and Baghdad and Breanna has to go to school!

This is what she has to say:

Breanna writes:

Getting to know the children of Baghdad has been an incredible privilege. Being able to Skype with them is a treasure. I'm honored that they take the time to know my name and find out about who I am. They eagerly look forward to speaking with me and earning trust with their new American friend. I value their friendship, much the way I value my friendship with Andrew White. One thing that I believe is amazing about them is how they worship and praise the Lord with everything going on around them. I care for the children in Baghdad as if they were my own siblings. I am so happy that I have this experience to get to know them.

There are four Norby children: Micaiah (17), Anna (15), Jacob (12) and Samuel (10). Micaiah is now in England helping me with my work before going on to university. Really, she is like a member of my family – I feel very protective towards her. In September 2009, David and some other members of the inner circle at St George's came to me after one of their regular private meetings and told me they had decided that, for the first time ever, a non-Iraqi was going to be allowed to join the inner circle: Micaiah. She was happy to do so, and now they talk to her even more than they did before. One day, they make it clear, they expect to see her. Maybe one day they will.

This is what the Norby children have to say:

Micaiah writes:

I have known Andrew for many years now. Over time, I have come to know him well and he has become a treasured family friend. In Andrew is the true heart of a father, which is apparent everywhere he goes. He stays in contact with people all over the world, and I am convinced that there are not many places he could go where he doesn't already know someone.

He lives an interesting life, one that most people probably couldn't cope with. Just being around him and seeing
his schedule of events and international trips, I doubt that I
could keep up with that kind of crazy life myself. The
amount of flying alone is incredible! Being afflicted with
MS doesn't make it any easier, as it leads to lack of sleep,
bad balance and poor health. Despite this, Andrew still
pushes through in Iraq with a joyful heart, because he
knows that God has called him to do this work. Seeing his
love for his friends and other people has taught me a lot:
how to persevere, how to be thankful and how to see the
big picture and ultimate goal in every situation.

Over the years it has always been a joy to greet him at
the Charlotte Douglas Airport and take him out for Thai
food – and then eat all the amazing English chocolates he
brings for us. I know that Andrew has always appreciated
coming to Charlotte, but sometimes it is surprising that he
finds so much joy in such a calm place, considering the
chaos of his usual surroundings. As a child, talking with
him in our living room, eating good food and sharing
stories, I don't think I ever truly understood the responsibil-
ity he carried or the trials he faced. He was always so
interested to hear about our schooling, our families and
our lives. I can't imagine how much was always on his
mind, all the important calls he had to make when he left
us for the day, all the troubles he had to deal with and the
things that left him with a lingering anxiety.

Since coming to England, I have gained a much larger
perspective of his life, and the trials of his work that he
never made apparent in his visits to us in the States. I can
see that visiting Charlotte is really a chance to escape from

everything he has to deal with day-to-day. Although we
are not children from a war zone or children in dire circum-
stances, he still loves us just as he loves them. I truly admire
Andrew for all he does and all he has accomplished. No
matter what happens he always pushes through, and I will
always consider him a dear friend.

Anna writes:

Knowing Andrew has been wonderful. I still remember the
first time we met. It was a conference at All Nations Church
and he talked to all of us kids and I remember thinking
how nice he was. Little did I know how big a part of our
life he would become! Now when he comes, all the youth
always run up and greet him with hugs. He is simply
amazing with kids and loves being with them.

Andrew has shown me a whole new side of Iraq. All you
hear in the news is tragedy, but he sees happiness and
good every day he is there. He tells us that not once has
any of the children at St George's asked, 'Why me? Why is
this happening to us?' I don't think I could ever really grasp
what they go through daily.

Over the year, we have made many 'friends' bracelets for
the children in Andrew's church in Baghdad and as we
make each one we pray over it for the person who is going
to get it. These bracelets are an important way we stay
connected to the children there.

Andrew White has a great impact wherever he goes.
God is always with him and everyone loves having him
around. I don't think I know another man like him.

Jacob writes:

Canon Andrew White is one of the nicest people I know. He has been visiting our church to preach for almost my whole life. He is very funny and rowdy – at my sister's graduation party he was speaking and singing in a Jamaican accent. Whenever he comes to Charlotte, we go to pick him up from the airport and then we go and eat out at a restaurant before he comes to our house. It is always a great time.

He is very generous and caring, and always gives us candy when he visits. He loves children, especially the ones at his church in Baghdad. We make bracelets for them and Andrew says these are their favorite thing in the world and when he asks them what they want, they say: 'More bracelets!'

He speaks at churches like ours in order to raise money for St George's Church and their medical clinic in Baghdad. He tells interesting stories, sometimes about the children in Iraq, sometimes about his office in England or about his kids. My life has been affected so much by knowing him – when he tells the inside scoop on what's happening in Iraq, it completely changes the way I look at the 'war on terror'. He talks about what is going on in Iraq, some of it terrible, like bombings, and some of it amazing, like the testimonies from his church. My favorite testimony is about how the Lord always provides for the congregation of that church, especially when they need it most.

I really enjoyed it when his two sons, Jacob and Josiah, visited from England over the Christmas break. They even got to be in our Christmas play. I hope Andrew can visit again soon.

Samuel writes:

Andrew is so funny and he is really great to be with.
I like making bracelets for him to take to the kids in
Baghdad.

Andrew tells us about how in Baghdad the bombs go off
and it is terrible but the children don't complain. Instead,
they pray that God will help them.

One day, I would like to go to Baghdad to meet the kids
there. I would like to see what they do there. Do they go
out a lot? Or do they mostly stay in the church?

I pray that Andrew will have the money to pay for all
the things they need at the church and that he will have a
great time there with the people.

Knowing Andrew has made my life better because
he helps me know God more. I really like it when he
comes here.

There are three Lane children: Josiah (18), Emily (16) and
Nathanael (11). Josiah has left school and is now training
with the air force, which gives me great joy. There is little I
could have wished for more for someone I am so close to
than to enter the American military, because (as I have said
many times before) they are today the greatest peacekeepers
in the world. One day, who knows, I could even end up
working with Josiah!

Josiah writes:

Bullets are flying, bombs are exploding. What man would
be crazy enough to walk straight in and talk to the head
terrorist? Canon Andrew White. This truly incredible international peace negotiator is the only man whom both
terrorists and military respect and listen to. As a British
citizen he has as much to fear from terrorists as anyone,
yet he is brave enough to arrange meetings and negotiate
with the most evil and deadly men alive. His courage to go
into war zones, when he has no military experience, and
his compassion for the downtrodden are truly inspiring.

The most obvious reason he is a hero is because of the
selfless courage he shows in resolving conflicts. He
describes his life as meetings with 'the bad guys and the
really, really bad guys'. In fact, when he saw the pack of
cards showing the '55 most wanted' people in Iraq at the
beginning of the war, he found that he knew most of them
– and yet those friendships are the only reason he has been
able to continue his never-ending work for peace there.

Furthermore, he is heroic in his incredible loyalty, which
goes hand-in-hand with his courage because he is, first of
all, loyal to God. In a land where many want to kill anyone
who worships God, not Allah, he remains true to his beliefs
and his morals. This gains him respect even from those who
want to kill him, and it is why Iraq's religious leaders trust
him enough to negotiate with him.

Andrew White defines the word 'hero', in that he risks
his life to bring hope to others without any desire for
recognition or reward. Ever since I met him seven years
ago, I have looked up to him and attempted to model my

life on his. He has taught me that if you trust in God, nothing is impossible. Furthermore, his love for everyone, good and bad, young and old, is undying and unstoppable. I am lucky to have been one of the people outside of the Middle East who has grown close with Andrew.

Emily writes:

Andrew White is one of the most incredible people I have ever met or observed. I first met him when I was about eight years old, when he was speaking at a church conference. I remember dancing to the music and stopping to stare at him because he radiated God's love. Throughout the day we kept running into each other, and he became my friend. That night I stayed up for hours making him a bracelet that said 'FRIENDS' because he was so kind to me that I wanted him to know. When I gave it to him the next morning he almost cried, because it was, he said, 'the first handmade gift I have ever received'. Later that day he told me about his job and some of the hardships the orphans in Iraq struggle with every day. His words and his personality touched me so greatly that we became fast friends, e-mailing frequently. My parents enthusiastically supported our friendship, due to the purity of Andrew's love and his passion for carrying out Jesus' will.

Shortly after his departure from the United States, we received an e-mail requesting as many 'friends' bracelets as we could make so that he could give them to his many children in Baghdad. My mom and I gladly did this to demonstrate the love the United States felt for them, and our prayers and support. What began as a small act of love has blossomed into a way of life that has resulted in the fruit of several thousand bracelets. I write this to show that the friendship between me and Andrew is a very real, blessed friendship that has influenced thousands of lives in the ways of Jesus' love.

When Andrew comes to All Nations, he is greeted with bear hugs from people young and old. It is a very beautiful sight because everyone is truly happy. Each time, it is a joyful reunion filled with people who wouldn't miss it for the world. When he is here we have as many small gatherings as possible to allow time and room for good food and fellowship. All are filled with laughter, brilliant conversations and the rekindling of relationships.

I do hope to be able to travel with Andrew some day, no matter how briefly, in order to see for myself the light in the darkness his church provides. I know it would change my life for ever to witness not only the terrible reality of life in Baghdad but also the way that his people join together in love, courage and determination to be the flower in the thorns. A visit to St George's Church would nurture the already strong bond I feel with them. They are truly an extension of my family, for when they hurt, I hurt and when they rejoice, I rejoice.

I truly admire Andrew, because he has been so courageous, persistent and selfless in all the facets of his life. Although he is afflicted with MS, and suffers the terrible penalty of being so often apart from those he loves, he will never cease his efforts to bring Jesus' peace to our corrupt world.

I value our friendship as one of the most important things I will ever possess. I constantly cover Andrew in prayer, especially focusing on healing, favour, protection and wisdom. I thank the Lord every day for allowing me the honor to call such a great man my friend.

Nathanael writes:

My first – and best – impression of Andrew was at a church conference when I was three. He was so big I thought he was a giant, yet he was so kind that all my fears melted away. After that, I just wanted to be his friend. I remember when he scooped me up and held me, I fell asleep in his lap because I felt so unbelievably safe. When he hugged me, I immediately felt peaceful.

When I discovered, many years later, that he ministers to many of those in distress in Baghdad, I knew he was the perfect person for this dangerous job. He is a father to all the Iraqi children in need, and a friend to all the widows. To me, he is the perfect father and friend as he is funny, happy and wise. He jokes with me and I know his smile comes from his heart. My family absolutely adores him and he is always welcome in our home and our lives. One of my favorite memories is of a time when Andrew came to our house and I showed him my room and we played games and just had fun.

We are honored to make bracelets for the children in Baghdad because it gives us an opportunity to influence their lives personally. I enjoy creating all the patterns and designs while taking the time to make them strong enough to endure their everyday struggles. Whenever Andrew's bracelet breaks or the color starts to wear off it, we make

him a new one. Seeing his smile inspires me to create
further bracelets for the children in Baghdad, whose lives
are far more challenging than mine. To meet these children
and become their friend is one of my greatest ambitions. I
am so joyful that they have someone to watch over them
as marvelous as Andrew. I truly love him!

Finally, there are three Decker children: Destiny (21),
Sophia (16) and Judah (10). I haven't asked them to write
for this book, but they are just as dear to me as the others.
Destiny is currently at Queens University of Charlotte,
majoring in political science (and focusing on the Middle
East), and she hopes to join me as an intern in England next
year.

CHAPTER 9

A Gift of the Holy Spirit

Wherever I am in the world, I think about my children every day. And when I say 'my children', I mean not just Josiah and Jacob but also my friends in Iraq, Israel, Palestine and America – to me they are all like my children. And as I think about them, I remember the words of Jesus recorded in Mark 10.13–16:

'People were bringing little children to Jesus to have him touch them, but the disciples rebuked them. When Jesus saw this, he was indignant. He said to them, "Let the little children come to me, and do not hinder them, for the kingdom of God belongs to such as these. I tell you the truth, anyone who will not receive the kingdom of God like a little child will never enter it."

'And he took the children in his arms, put his hands on them and blessed them.'

As I reflect on these wonderful words, I see that our Lord, too, loved children. His followers might have rebuked those who brought them to him, but Jesus did not – he wanted them. Perhaps he even needed them, as I do. The key to his relationship with them was very simple. It was – and is still – all about love: a love without limit, a love for which all children, and especially those in places afflicted by conflict, cry out.

A few weeks ago, a little boy of eight came up to me at St George's and said, '*Abuna*, will you be my daddy?' His father had been one of Saddam's ministers and had been arrested and tried and executed. This man was a Muslim but his wife is a Christian and she so wanted their son to be brought up as a Christian. We had to take him into the Green Zone to baptize him secretly. When he asked me to be his daddy, it really hurt me and at the same time it made me determined to give him anything and everything he needs. I put my arms around him and said: 'You can be my boy. I'll always love you.' All he wanted was to be able to tell everyone that he does have a dad. There are quite a few other children at the church in the same situation as him and I am only too glad to say yes to them as well. I don't find it onerous: I am quite a big man and there is plenty of me to go round! If anything, it bothers me that they feel they need to ask me to be their daddy – I wish they all took it for granted that I will be.

However, Jesus did not call the children to him only because he wanted to express his love for them. He also wanted the adults to see what they should learn from them. The truth is that children have a wonderful capacity not only to receive love but also to feel it and express it. In the Green Zone in Baghdad, it is very rare that you see any children, and those who work there often long to see some. Children are all the more delightful when you are starved of contact with them. When we have our weekly meetings at the hotel al-Rashid of members of my two congregations, St George's and the Coalition chapel, it is the children that the soldiers and diplomats most want to see. For their part, the children are eager to see the grown-ups from the Coalition, because it's so obvious how much these foreigners adore them!

I believe that the open and endless love these children seem to have for everybody is important not just to those of us connected with the Coalition but to all the people of Iraq. We often say in Iraq, 'We have lost everything and all we have left is Jesus,' and for us one part of Jesus is the love we experience from his little children. They, too, have lost so much, yet Jesus still shines through them. And yet so many people, like the disciples in the Gospel, see children as a nuisance and a burden, not a blessing, because they prevent the adults from doing what they want to in the way they want to. It worries me when I see so many churches today that say they are 'pro children' but don't really allow them to be part of a worshipping community.

In so many ways, I find that children are doing the work of God's kingdom in ways that adults find very difficult. Maybe it is because many of them are not aware of all the complexities of what is going on around them. Maybe it is because they have a very simple faith in God and love for him. The older children who are close to me remind me that in everything I am trying to be and do I am doing the work of my Lord: opposing the Evil One and his powers of darkness and demonstrating the love of the Father. This is the work of God's kingdom, which extends his heavenly rule. And in essence this is the work of love – as we say in Arabic each week at St George's: '*Al-Hubb, al-Hubb, al-Hubb*' ('[We must] love, love, love'). Is this not what Jesus meant when he said that unless we become like little children we will never enter God's kingdom?

There is so much in the Christian faith that goes against the grain of our culture, and the status of children is a prime example. Our society teaches us that children are merely adults-in-waiting, who don't really count until they have grown up and who must be encouraged to do so as fast as possible. Our faith, mysteriously, tells us rather that these little people have a role of their own already and insists that unless we ourselves possess certain of their traits we won't even be able to enter God's kingdom. If ever you wonder what it means to live as a Christian, look at those children who love Jesus! We can learn simply from them. As Rodney Howard-Browne said to me, I have 'seen God' in children – and it is something I will never forget.

I am not saying simplistically that we don't need to grow up. 1 Corinthians 13.11 makes it clear that we do: 'When I was a child, I talked like a child, I thought like a child, I reasoned like a child. When I became a man, I put childish ways behind me.' We all understand the need to grow up – and yet at the same time we have a need to hold on to the innocence and simplicity of childhood. I have said many times in public that I start my prayers each night in exactly the same way I did when I was three years old. The fact that he manifests himself so clearly in the young, the weak and the unsophisticated demonstrates the nature of God, who is strong and yet allowed himself to experience weakness and to suffer and die on the cross. If we (be)come like little children, we can enter into the very nature of his rule, which is loving kindness; and this means we can share in the benefits of his kingdom. Without them, we will struggle even to live as followers of Jesus.

As I look at the many children at St George's, I can see that their faith in our Lord is profound. One day I sat down with some of them and asked them: 'What does Jesus mean to you?' They told me that they love Jesus so much because he loves them so much. There was no doubt about this in their minds. He was always with them – and especially when things were bad, when bombs were falling and they had to hide under the table. They talked a lot about the Cross: their understanding of Jesus centred on the fact that he had died for them. I asked those of them who had lost loved ones what they thought of Jesus, and their response was even stronger. They had no doubt that their loved ones were with him and that they were all speaking Aramaic together.

I remembered some words I learned at theological college, from a lecture given by the late Professor James Torrance. They are used at baptisms in the French Reformed Church, when the pastor takes the child in his arms and says: 'Little child, for you Christ has suffered the terror of Gethsemane and the agony of Calvary, for you he has cried "It is finished" and for you, little child, even though you do not realize it, the gospel becomes true: we love him because he first loved us.' These are not words from any Anglican liturgy, but I confess I have used them in every child baptism I have done since I completed my curacy. It is these words that sum up for me the unique relationship between our Lord and his children. It is these words I use in Baghdad. It is these words I recall when I see how its children suffer.

The children of Charlotte and Baghdad may live totally different lives in totally different places and cultures, but the things they have in common are all that matters: that they are children and that they love Jesus and know he loves them. Differences in churchmanship mean nothing to them – most of them don't even know they exist. I'll never forget the day when the chair of my Foundation, Lord Hylton, came to St George's. He wrote an article afterwards in which he said: 'I have been to the church of the future.' What did he mean? He meant a church where denominations do not matter. Our church is full of people of all denominations – there are only three Anglicans in it, including me! The fact that its congregation is so different from that of All Nations doesn't matter. We are one – and it's the children who make this oneness so real. Children do not understand what it means to be Catholic, Orthodox or Anglican, Strict Baptist or Pentecostal. All that matters to them is that you love Jesus.

(It does help at St George's, though, if you also love Jonah and Mar Thoma, as they were the two evangelists who brought the true faith to this part of the world. Jonah persuaded the citizens of Nineveh [on the edge of modern-day Mosul] to believe in the God of Abraham, Isaac and Jacob, and Thomas stopped off in the same city, on his way to India, and told them their Messiah had come. To this day, most of Iraq's Christians come from this region. Their children know and love these stories that they have all been brought up on. Jonah and Thomas may be two of the most miserable people in the Bible, but to the Christian children of Iraq they are heroes!)

In these respects, I find that the children I know are prophetic. What they do not do, I have found, is ask the kinds of penetrating question people sometimes expect from children: 'Why do there have to be wars? Why can't people all live together in peace?' Most American and British children have never witnessed war and, in my experience, they tend to think that 'if it's good for our country, it can't be bad'. The children of Iraq, on the other hand, have never known anything other than conflict and bloodshed. In a strange way, the fact that these things have always been the norm for them means that they remain connected with normality in a way that most adults in Iraq are not. They have all witnessed horrors of a kind that few children in Britain or America will ever see – and yet their lives do not seem to be dominated and dictated by the danger of the moment.

Sometimes, they can seem almost blasé about it. A week before Christmas 2009, David and Lina went to get some pizza for the inner circle. They were gone for quite some time, and when they eventually returned they told us that no sooner had they left the pizza shop than it had been blown up. It didn't appear to have dampened their spirits, and the party continued with the usual joy, going on long after I had gone to bed. When I asked David and Lina why the bomb didn't seem to have troubled them, they laughed and said they had bombs every day. It was just part of the daily routine, David told me: 'breakfast, lunch, dinner and bombs.' They were so matter-of-fact about it! If you are constantly surrounded by violence, I suppose you have to close your mind to it. Even when you are directly affected by it, you can find ways to blank out the fear, the pain or the grief. I will never forget one little Iraqi boy called Muhammad whom I saw in a hospital in Amman. He had been hit in the neck by a stray American bullet and had been left quadriplegic. Apart from his head, he could move nothing. And yet he never complained. Sometimes people ask me why I am not more analytical about what is happening in Iraq, and I think the answer may be that I simply cannot afford to think too much about these things. If I were to dwell too much on the traumas and terrors of Baghdad, perhaps it would prevent me from wanting to go back.

The truth is, however, that even now the prospects for the children of Iraq are not good. Even those who are physically unscathed must be psychologically damaged. Today, almost 40 per cent of the population are younger than 15 years old. According to the Iraqi Ministry of Labour and Social Affairs, at the beginning of 2008 there were something like 4.5 million 'orphans' – by which it meant prepubescent children who had lost their fathers at least. Half a million of these were then living on the streets. These figures are not reliable, but they are certainly believable. In a population of some 29 million, this is a huge, huge problem. Women who have been widowed in Iraq are unlikely ever to get employment. Their daughters have a bleak future. Their sons are easy prey for both the militias and criminal gangs, and many turn to violence or substance abuse or both. Even if peace were to come to Iraq tomorrow, the social problems stored up for the future of this country are simply immense.

Nonetheless, as I have often said, I have hope. It is not political; it is spiritual. It is summed up in the words of Edward Mote's famous hymn 'My Hope is Built on Nothing Less':

My hope is built on nothing less
Than Jesus' blood and righteousness;
I dare not trust the sweetest frame,
But wholly lean on Jesus' name.
On Christ, the solid Rock, I stand;
All other ground is sinking sand.

It is this kind of hope that is understood and shared by the children. They do not place any trust in either the Iraqi government or the Coalition, but only in the One who said, 'Let the little children come to me.' And they do come to him. Without Jesus there is no hope for them. With him, there is every hope. They know they are loved and valued. They know that they matter, not just to me but to God. At the same time, their love, for Jesus and for each other, and the faith that sustains them give me real hope – and vision for the future, too. In this respect, too, they are prophetic, a witness to Iraq and to the world. Everybody around them may lose heart, many may have doubts; but for them their God is always the same, 'yesterday, today and for ever'. It is easy to talk about such ideas but to see them lived out is a different matter.

Recently, I asked the inner circle at St George's to tell me about their faith. They talked about how Jesus, the Son of God, had shed his blood for them – 'Not like Muhammad,' one of them added. Then they started talking about all the hardships they were enduring. They said that life had to be difficult because Jesus said that it would be before his return. Iraq's present troubles were for them a sign that their Lord is coming back very soon.

What they said next rather surprised me. It made me acutely aware of how significant my words are to them –

sometimes as they explained things to me I could have imagined I was listening to myself! They started talking about the last three verses of Isaiah 19. Speaking all at once, they told me about the highway that will run from Iraq (in Isaiah's day, Assyria) through Israel to Egypt. Then they told me about what was happening today in those three countries. As far as they were all concerned, their land is God's land. They asked me why all the other churches were not teaching people about this passage, and I said simply that soon more of them would be.

Then they moved on to another crucial subject that I often speak about: love. They talked about how much God loves them, and then went on to say that loving God means that you also need to love other people, even your enemies. David remarked that he had always been told that the Americans were evil, but when he was with them he had seen how lovely they were. I explained that loving American soldiers was not quite the same as loving your enemies. Fulla said that their enemies were the people who planted the bombs that had recently struck St George's.[5] All the children agreed that it was difficult to love the people who were responsible for such things, but they insisted that they were

5   In August 2009, a bomb had shattered all the windows in the church. Two months later, a few hours before the Sunday morning service, two large explosions had hit the building even more powerfully, blowing in the doors and even the window frames and destroying most of the equipment in the clinic. On the streets outside, 164 people had been killed and many fragments of human bodies were found inside the church. Mercifully, there had been no one inside St George's when its interior was sprayed with shards of glass. Six weeks later, another blast had shaken the church (and another had blown David off his feet as he was returning home from the office of Mar Immanuel Deli).

really trying. They assured me that the love inside their hearts was real love that God had given them to share with everybody.

Finally, they talked about peacemaking. They quoted the beatitude 'Blessed are the peacemakers, for they will be called sons of God,' and said: 'We are the children of a "peace daddy"' – meaning me – 'so we are also about peacemaking.' They said that they are all children of God, because they take after their 'daddy'. (This is a very Middle Eastern point of view, that what your father is, you will be too.)

These children are for me a gift of the Holy Spirit. I have seen more of the miraculous in Iraq than anywhere else, and it is so often children who are the channels for it. It is they and their young friends in America who give me inspiration, constant love and hope for the future – even when there seems to be no hope. When all around me is violence and destruction, it is the young – who are least to blame and have most to lose, but are least considered or consulted by the powers that be – who remind me that things can be different, that what is broken can be repaired and restored. They take my eyes off what is temporal and corrupted and direct them towards what is eternal and incorruptible. It is they who enable me to bring God into what is godless.

Suddenly, prayer becomes real. For me, they are the vehicle for the presence of the Almighty. When I am with them, I no longer feel that I am struggling alone to do the impossible: I remember that through God all things are possible. In children there is such simple trust and faith that often I go to them and ask simply, 'Will you come and pray with me?' They always do, and our prayers are always answered. When an American friend of mine was critically ill recently, it was the children who came and prayed for him every day. And when he was discharged from hospital, we had a party.

In the midst of the darkness that so often surrounds me, it is the children who cause light to shine. Whether my work for peace will finally bear fruit, I don't know; but I do know that I could not do it if it were not for them. I will always give thanks for them. As he loves them, may our Lord bless them and protect them!